The Dolls' House

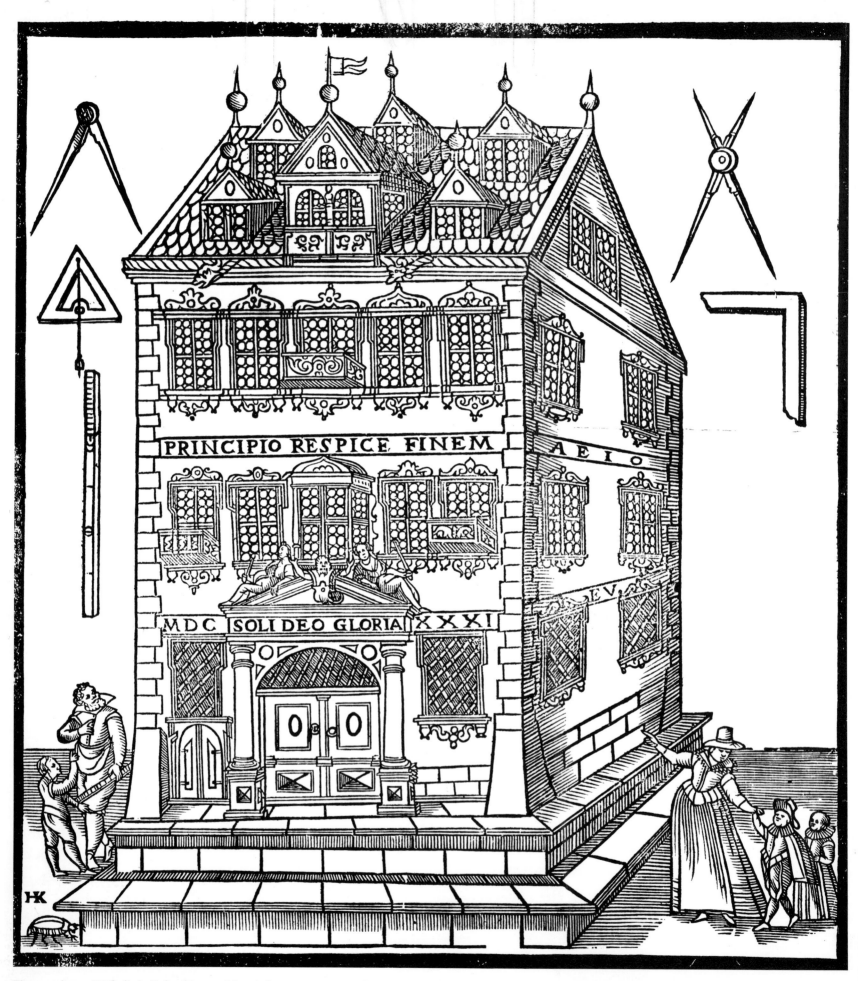

Fig. 1   Anna Köferlin's Baby House. Nuremberg, 1631. Woodcut, signed HK.

Leonie von Wilckens

The Dolls' House

An Illustrated History

BELL & HYMAN
London

First published in 1980 by
BELL & HYMAN LIMITED
Denmark House
37–39 Queen Elizabeth Street
London SE1 2QB

First published by
Verlag Georg D.W. Callwey, Munich
Translated by Anna R.E.K. Meuss, M.T.G., F.I.L.
Photographs by Helga Schmidt-Glassner

British Library Cataloguing in Publication Data

Wilckens, Leonie von
The dolls' house.
1. Doll-houses – History
I. Title   II. Mansions in miniature
688.7'23'0903   NK4894.A2

ISBN 0 7135 1238 5

Printed in Spain by
Mateu Cromo Artes Gráficas, S.A
Pinto (Madrid)

Contents

Note: Numbers in margins (pages 7-63):
Numbers in heavy type indicate Figures, numbers in light type indicate Plates.

Preface by Vivien Greene

It was my privilege to have met Dr von Wilckens in 1959, though it was not my initial visit to the Germanische Museum, one of the four greatest museums of the Western world, and she is still guardian of that incomparable Department devoted to toys and to the magnificent Nürnberg Baby Houses. Reading this book one may guess that these, of all the treasures in her care, are the nearest to her heart because they show in microcosm the social history – habits, possessions, luxuries and hardships – of a period which has engrossed her so deeply. Her descriptions of these interiors are riveting. Here she shows the meticulous care of her research, centred particularly on the kitchens (always the most interesting room in any house!) and storerooms: their brass and pewter, the bread oven, the chickens in a pen in the corner, the coffee-roasters and the dumpling-pans: she makes us almost hear the bustle and clamour of a large, self-supporting household of the seventeenth and eighteenth centuries.

Her scholarship can perhaps only be appreciated fully by those who have themselves spent time in research: few others can guess at the regrets when facts which have taken months to accumulate have to be discarded because they clutter the general effect or detract from an exploration more relevant; and again, apprehension that records fascinating to the writer may bore the reader: the choices to be made, the loss perhaps of a precious and irreplaceable notebook – all this may lie behind the confident exposition of such a book as this, on a theme so little explored, in this case the Continental Baby Houses.

Each reader will find a favourite section: may I recommend 'Cupboards of All Kinds' with the entrancing descriptions of 'cloak-woods' (i.e. coat-hangers) and the ingenious arrangements for hanging the wide-hooped skirts so that they remained uncreased. These arrangements of course were of a very early date, mid-seventeenth century, earlier than any English Baby House.

It is diverting to note the furnishings, some totally unknown here, in these Continental houses; the practical washbasin, for instance, hanging on the wall with its water container above it, the wall-holders for dusters and – above all – the innumerable cooking implements! It was particularly frustrating to be unable to discover their purpose – some Curators, even, could not explain how they were used, for most had been obsolete for two hundred years. At that time (I am still referring to the 1950s) there was of course little interest in Baby Houses, with the noble exception of the Germanische. I remember walking through room after room – were there sixty? – in Munich to see the only exhibit to my purpose, a small case in one section of which lay some miniature silverware for a dolls' house. The generous and sympathetic Curator, however, allowed me to explore the basement where the houses and toy furniture were stored, and I was locked in for a winter's day to unpack alone and to make notes on the most superb seventeenth and eighteenth century miniature furniture, including mirrors and framed oil-paintings on copper, all wrapped in dusty yellowed newspapers dated 1938–9. It is certain that these lovely things are now on display.

Having experienced the joy of visiting every Museum mentioned in this book, (Bologna and Hamburg excepted) I can with enthusiasm assure the reader that to learn from the scholarship unfolded here and to study the splendid photographs is the experience closest to confronting these treasures in actuality. The historical information is unobtainable anywhere else, of course, and the details shown are better seen in the photographs than in the original houses themselves.

VIVIEN GREENE

Cabinets of Curiosities

The Baby House of Duke Albert V of Bavaria

More than four hundred and twenty years ago, in 1557–58, Duke Albert V of Bavaria had a Baby House made[1], a project involving considerable expenditure. Albert, Duke of Bavaria from 1550 to 1579, undoubtedly gave detailed directions as to how the house was to be designed and furnished. The result was a miniature replica, as we shall see, of the house of a Southern German prince of that period. From the nineteenth-century this, the earliest known example, was considered to be the precursor of the innumerable dolls' houses that have been produced since, an opinion that continues to be widely held to the present day. In fact, however, this is a misapprehension.

Ten years later, Albert V commissioned Jacob Sandtner, a master turner from Straubing, to carve scale models of his five official residences, the towns of Straubing, Landshut, Munich, Ingolstadt and Burghausen[2]. The Baby House was thus followed by the replicas of towns in which it might well have stood, a secure dwelling place. Between 1563 and 1567, William Egkl erected a separate building in the Old Yard *(Alter Hof)* in Munich, the Mint Yard *(Münzhof)* of today, to house the Duke's 'cabinet'. Here, in the first museum to be established north of the Alps, the five model towns and the Baby House were displayed. They are listed and described in considerable detail in the 1598 inventory of the ducal cabinet. The Munich House was clearly not designed to be a children's toy, but rather as a cabinet piece, like the five model towns, to be looked at and admired, a complete house, faithfully presenting the architecture and furnishings of a princely dwelling, just as the towns show the general layout and full exterior details of every building.

Many craftsmen contributed to the Munich House, some local and some from other places. Names that have come down to us are those of the court joiner Wolf Greiss, the locksmiths Hans Klein and Kaspar Bauer, and also the painters Hans Ostendorfer and Hans Schöpfer the Elder. The Bavarian Duke was married to Anne of Austria, sister of Archduke Ferdinand of the Tyrol (1529–95) who built Ambras Castle near Innsbruck to house the fabulous treasures he had accumulated since 1547[3] - weapons, works of art, antiquities and curiosities of all kinds, today the pride of the Viennese Collections. Even now, visitors to Ambras are enchanted with the remnants to be found there of the former 'Cabinet of Curiosities and *Wunderkammer*' intrigued by the remarkable variety of objects, the precision of the work of artist-craftsmen, the amazingly wide range of finds and inventions. The background to the Baby Houses of the 16th and 17th centuries is, therefore, a period of princes and great lords creating Mannerist and Early Baroque collections, a passion soon shared also by the well-to-do burghers of the free imperial cities and of Dutch trading towns. Then as now, they reflected pride of possession. It was the acquisitive instinct, the desire to possess and collect, which led to their creation. The miniature of a well-organized household was produced to show what possessions one held, how one lived, just as Albert V wished to have his country represented by his five official residences. The Baby Houses certainly were not children's toys; that is, toys as they came to be known in the nineteenth and twentieth centuries—things specially designed for children, to entertain them and keep them occupied.

In those days, children were regarded as small, as yet imperfect, adults who needed to learn how to conduct themselves in adult life. They were constantly instructed how to act and behave as adults. To allow them to be children in their own right, to say 'children are different' was a totally unknown concept, as were toys created specially for children. A doll, even a simple one made of clay or carved from wood and painted, would be a miniature version of a lady or a woman. Of course, children have always had the imagination to let simple bits of wood, often showing little semblance of form, become a doll or other childish plaything. But one can hardly describe these as toys in the modern sense. Norbert Elias[4] refers only to 'boys', but one could say quite generally that children in both the sixteenth and seventeenth centuries, 'even if in service, if socially dependent, lived from a very early age in the same social sphere as adults'. The 'distance between the behavioural and affective standards of adults and children' was less marked. 'Again and again one can see how our understanding of earlier as well as of our present-day psychology depends very much on paying closer attention to the way in which this distance developed, to the gradual emergence of a special and separate sphere in which human beings gradually came to spend the first twelve, fifteen, and now almost twenty years of their life. Biological development must have been very much the same then as now, but we need to consider this social change if we really want to get closer understanding of the whole problem complex of 'being grown-up' as it presents itself today . . .'

The term 'Dockenhaus' (Baby House) was obviously considered in the nineteenth century to indicate that the 1558 Munich House was a toy made for the Duke's children. However, the term 'dolls' house' or Baby House only came to be used to refer to a toy in the late eighteenth and early nineteenth centuries, when concepts began to change as to childhood mentality, parallel to new developments in the education of children. Before that, the attributive use of 'doll' or 'baby' referred to the fact that the object was reproduced to a smaller scale.

Unfortunately the 1558 House was lost when the Munich residence burned down in 1674. However, the detailed description given in the inventory of the ducal cabinet, a document written in 1598 by Johann Baptist Fickler[5], Court Councillor to the Duke, provides an excellent picture of the Baby House and its contents. It is also important to realize that in the model Manor Farm which the learned merchant and

art dealer Philip Hainhofer of Augsburg had made between 1610 and 1617, together with the famous Pomeranian Cabinet, for Duke Philip II of Pomerania-Stettin[6], the domestic sections were no doubt closely related to those of the Munich House, though somewhat more sophisticated, with a clock that struck the hour and birds that sang. As it went with the Pomeranian Cabinet, the Manor Farm, also no longer in existence, never really came to be regarded as a (toy) dolls' house. A detailed study of the Munich Baby House will also inevitably lead one to recognize its real nature, as an object for display among the works in a cabinet of curiosities. The 1598 description was published in 1879[7]. Translated into modern language it reads:

'The Baby House is four stories high. The ground floor has five doors and fifteen windows, the first floor four doors and sixteen windows, the second three doors and sixteen windows, the third five doors and sixteen windows. The ground floor consists of a stable with three stalls, each containing a carved wooden horse. A rider is mounted on the horse that is in front, and there is a stablehand beside each of the other two; a feed-box stands by the wall, a stablehand beside it; also three saddles and headgear. Next to the stable is a byre, and in it three cows, a calf, a milkmaid, a feed-box; the mistress of the house stands by a table with dairy equipment. At the back of the stable is the dairy and in it a maid making butter; all kinds of household things of wood and copper hang on the wall or stand against it. After the byre comes the larder; there, all kinds of game are hanging on the walls, both winged and four-legged; on a table are some dishes and small wooden troughs, with a prepared pig's head, a capon, a goose, a lamb, a wood-grouse, a kid, a sheep's head, a Westphalian ham and a platter of sausages; at the very back of the larder is a killed stag and another animal, also a calf with its feet bound; the house-steward and a manservant stand beside a food cupboard. The larder is followed by the wine-cellar and in it six large wine barrels for herb-flavoured wine; also a table, on which there are four hand-baskets, large and small, of silver-wire; furthermore four ewers, a cauldron, a large round-bellied ewer, all of silver; behind the table, six silver bottles hang on the wall. Stairs go up one wall to the house above. Under the stairs are all kinds of bottles, jugs and ewers of glass. After the cellar comes the coach house; it contains a carriage, its body covered in black velvet and suspended in the frame; also a small carriage for the ladies, again velvet-covered, and with silver-mounted wheels.

'First floor: First a bathroom; here the mistress of the house and three daughters are taking their baths, a maidservant is in attendance; also a bath tub, two copper tubs, a copper bailer, two barber's pots of gilded brass, two gilded washing bowls. In front of the bathroom is a small dressing room with a made-up bed, its cover of black velvet brocade; further a table with velvet cover and embroidered tablecloth; on the table an embroidered shift and a number of embroidered kerchiefs and handkerchiefs together with a brush, the handle of which is covered in velvet and mounted with silver; furthermore a silver drying hat (drying stand) with three gilded feet; beside the table sits a woman in a black silk dress with a belt of silver wire. Two large and ten small gilded brass washing bowls and three bath hats are hanging on the wall behind her. After the bathroom comes the kitchen. On the hearth are several spits with poultry and other roasts and a number of pots; the man-cook is skimming the soup. Another cook stands at the bench. He is dressing a capon in a copper vessel. On the other side, a cook is hanging meat. On the dresser are eleven large pewter dishes with etched decorations, also seven smaller dishes similarly ornamented, and five pewter platters. There the master of the kitchen stands, cutting open a pike. Two large fishes lie in a copper cooling-kettle; beside it is a small fish-kettle made of tinplate, a three-legged silver casserole ('*Tortenpfanne*'[8] = baking pan) with appurtenances, three copper casseroles, a copper water container and another copper vessel. All kinds of kitchen implements made from copper, brass and pewter are hanging on the walls, and a brass mortar, a pair of bellows and a number of other items of the kind one would expect to find in a well-organized kitchen are arranged on a rack. Next to the kitchen is the yard, at its centre a hexagonal fountain with a figure cast in metal. At the back are two chicken coops, one on top of the other, and a poultry run. In the corner of the yard is a small barred lion house with a lion and a lioness. A garden with trees comes after the yard. The trellis around three sides of it is overgrown with vines and roses. In this garden are a stag, two deer, a dog, a cat, lizards, slow-worms and other beasts; on a long bench are six silver flowerpots with red and white carnations and other plants in them. In the middle of the garden is a silver draw-well with two silver buckets. All the trees and plants in the garden are of meshwork ('glissmater').

'On the second floor: first a ballroom where the prince and princess are sitting under a canopy of brown satin embroidered in silver. On the roof of the canopy are the arms of Bavaria with those of Austria incorporated. There are four fiddlers, three dancing couples – young nobles and ladies in garments of satin and taffeta. On one side, the governess in a gown of black velvet and three maids of honour in gowns of red satin embroidered in gold and with silvergilt belts, such as the dancing ladies are also wearing. Before them is a long table with four silver legs, its cover of red satin. On the table is the game known as nine-holes ('*zum Narren*'[9]); its stand and balls are of silver. Four equerries and two pages of the court are standing beside the prince and princess; next to them, spiral stairs lead to the room above. The ballroom is followed by a parlour, its walls covered in gold brocade. The duke and duchess are in the parlour, with four ladies of the court and six servants, dressed in black and brown satin, with petticoats of white satin; beside the stove stands the jester. In the middle of this room is a rectangular table with a brocade cover; on it lie a gilded wooden lute and two Indian bells. A silvergilt cage hangs above the table, with a parrot. Against the side wall is a cupboard covered with red double taffeta; on it are a silvergilt flagon, two ewers, three double goblets, twelve goblets with lids, on tall feet, an open-work, partly gilded censer on a small four-legged square plate, a wash-hand basin and ewer, four shallow sugar dishes, two plates, all of gilded silver. Next to the cupboard are three small hanging cupboards with painted doors. Near to the ladies is a little dog covered in white floss silk instead of skin, two others that are similar, and a very small one also of floss silk; besides an English dog with a silver-mounted collar, on it a double A with the Bavarian and Austrian coats of arms.

'After the parlour comes a chamber with a made-up bed; the pillows and linen are embroidered in red silk, the brocade covers decorated with red satin appliqué. The curtains and valances around the bed are of red satin bordered with embroidered brocade. Before the bed lies an embroidered carpet that looks like a Turkey one. The princess is sitting in a brocade-covered chair beside the bed, and there is also the governess in a black satin gown trimmed with gold. On a chest beside her, inlaid and with gilded mountings, lies a linen cloth with many decorative seams and embroidered with gold thread, also a night-cap with gold edging decorated in the same manner, a kerchief and a handkerchief similarly embellished with rows of stitching and gold lace, a mouth veil bordered in black silk and with gold lace, a handkerchief embroidered in black silk and with rows of ornamental stitches, and finally a man's shirt decorated with embroidery in black silk. Before the bed, a silver pot and a pair of velvet indoor slippers. At the foot of the bed is a chair covered in red velvet with a red velvet cushion. Along the wall facing the bed, a long table, its cover

decorated with embroidery in red silk and with a fringe all around. On the table, a large and a small basket made from silver wire, a fire screen for delicate ladies to hold in front of them when they stand before the hearth, that the heat of the fire may not spoil their delicate faces; a wash-hand basin and ewer of silver, etched and partly gilded, a silver vessel with gilded decorations, a silver tankard, an oval silver box with two gilded rings of Parisian workmanship, a hairbrush with a silver handle.

'On the third and uppermost floor: first the chapel, with the altar in front, the altar piece carved and painted; on the altar a cloth of white double taffeta, embroidered all over with gold and silver thread; the altar hangings of black velvet, in front the name of Jesus, like the edges embroidered in silver. Upon the altar a silvergilt crucifix, two silver candlesticks with gilt decorations, a silvergilt chalice with paten, a silvergilt corporal, two silver cruets with gilded decorations, a silver bell with gilded decorations, a silver thurifer with aspergil, also with gilded decorations. On each of the altar shelves to the right and to the left a two-handled silver jug holding roses worked in mesh. A priest is standing before the altar, beside him the gospel and the epistle reader, their chasubles and dalmatics of brocade. Beside the altar a virginal (keyboard instrument), its lid closed. At the centre of the chapel, on a desk covered with red double taffeta, a hymnbook bound in red satin, with silver mounts, for the bass. Six choristers in long coats of black wool edged with velvet are standing behind the desk. On another desk covered with red double taffeta that is standing next to them against the wall, lies a hymnbook similar to the one already described, for the contralto; next to it are two more, for tenor and soprano, and four small hymnbooks bound in black. Adjoining the chapel is a small room from where the duke and duchess follow the service. After the chapel comes a chamber, its walls covered in red silk damask patterned in yellow; in it are three made-up beds with covers, curtains

Fig. 2 *Title* page from *Newes Modelbuch* by Johann Sibmacher. Nuremberg, 1604.

and valances of red double taffeta, edged in red velvet. A wooden chest on four feet is covered with framed enamel plates and lined with fine red taffeta. A winged chair for two people, turned work, is covered in red velvet. By the second bed is an ivory chamber pot. The chamber is followed by a parlour where two noblewomen are sitting, one with her work cushion; their gowns are of black silk trimmed with gold. By the stove, a woman is spinning, with a distaff. The walls of this parlour are covered in gold silk work with a diamond pattern. A rectangular table has a cover in the same material; a weaving frame and a small spinning wheel are standing in front of it. A small sewing box beside the table contains skeins of red and blue silk, needle and thread, a thimble and small fasteners; the box bears the arms of Brandenburg and of Wuerttemberg; another small box is painted all around. A mirror in an ivory frame hangs on the wall by the table. On the other side of the room is a cupboard completely covered with the silk material that has already been mentioned; on it are a knife-case, three small tumblers, two tall goblets with lids, two drinking cups, a tall round-bellied goblet with lid, a glass cut from white chalcedony, two candlesticks, a dish, eight plates, a wash-hand basin with fountain, all made of ivory. After the parlour comes a kitchen; on the hearth, a silver roasting spit with a 'firedog' for turning the spit; a wild duck is impaled on the spit; two green glazed pots stand by the fire. On the dresser are six pewter dishes with handles, nine plain pewter dishes, six pewter platters, seven pewter plates; all kinds of kitchen implements are hanging on the two walls: brass and copper pans, also small tubs of sheet metal, and other items large and small; there is also a copper water vessel, a cooling kettle and a water container. The kitchen is followed by a nursery with a small chamber; the nursery walls are covered in a red material interwoven with silver. A woman in a silk dress is standing by the stove, beside her a small boy in velvet frock and red hose; in the foreground, a woman, also garbed in velvet, is rocking a child in a hanging cradle. There is also a young maiden in a gown of red satin, trimmed with gold and silver, and in a high chair a child dressed in a short shift. Behind the woman rocking the child, a rectangular table with a red velvet cover may be seen, on it a small chest with pewter-plated iron fastenings and within this all kinds of linen made of finely embroidered lawn; the chest is painted gold outside. Also three sewing baskets made of silver wire, a silver vessel with gilded decorations, a small dog covered in white floss silk. A cupboard with a red double taffeta cover is standing against the wall next to the stove, on it are a tall hospitality cup with lid, six court cups, a mounted nutmeg with a lid, five bowls, four candlesticks, a wash-hand basin with ewer, five small candlesticks, three small cups, two small three-legged cups, twelve plates, all of silver. A silver-handled brush and a silver pan are hanging on the wall by the cupboard. In the chamber next to the nursery, two beds are made up, their valances and curtains of gold-embroidered lawn have golden fringes.'

Such sumptuous furniture and fittings, in silk and satin, brocade, velvet, embroidered in gold and silk, with many items produced by craftsmen, cannot have been designed with children in mind. They provided a picture of a noble princely household and were made to be admired and to impress. At Torgau Castle in 1572, the three children of August Elector of Saxony were given a hunt and many household things[10] for Christmas, a gift arranged by Hieronymus Rauscher, mayor of Leipzig. But again the furniture, table linen, household, table and kitchen equipment undoubtedly were not intended as playthings, but to furnish a house as an object lesson for the future mistresses and ladies of princely houses, to instruct them about running a house and all it involved. The point is not specifically made on this occasion, but considering the attitudes of those times, that is how it must have been.

The Manor Farm for Duke Philip II of Pomerania-Stettin

Excerpts from a description of the Manor Farm Hainhofer had made for the Pomeranian duke[11], again rewritten in more modern language, may serve to demonstrate that both the Munich and the Stettin Houses had a similar function, i.e. as cabinet pieces.

'On the other side, one enters the larder; at the top, twelve glass vessels containing all kinds of delectable waters, beneath them twelve earthen plates, six tubs, plate cases, pewter bowls and plates, white earthern jars, bread, candles, provisions suspended from hooks; two maids, one of them cutting lard, the other chopping meat, a pair of scales with weights. As one leaves the larder and ascends the stairs, the everyday parlour is on the right; here the lady of the house is sitting at a rectangular table covered with a green cloth, she is sewing; the nursery maid walks the child in leading reins that teases the cat with a rag on a string; also a cupboard, a washing box, both with glasses, cups, spoon, two-pronged fork (for serving), knife, linen and other items. A lazy-bed (popular for taking a rest during the day), chairs, distaff, board game, on the wall a mirror and a calendar. From the parlour one enters the chamber, its walls hung with tapestries; in it is a made-up bed with green taffeta curtains and lovely bedding. A child is asleep in its cot. Beside this stands a press with four doors, with the silver stored at the top and the linen below. Two chests of garments, on the wall a sword, cross-belt and dagger, on a small table a night-candle. Two young ladies are sitting in a passage and sewing, beside them a parrot and a dressed-up monkey on a chain. In the kitchen, a maid stands by the open hearth, cooking pap for the child. There one finds all the things needed in a kitchen. In a food cupboard, beside which a black cat is reaching for a fish in a tub, are green and white pots, pans of copper, brass and iron, dishes, plants, candlesticks, squirts, spoons, roasting spit, water barrel, vegetables, a chopping block for meat, fish jars. Sausages are hanging in the chimney, and fire pumps on the kitchen and parlour doors. Going up the stairs one immediately enters the hall. In it is a long table, with a red velvet cloth, the cloth can be removed, table and chairs moved aside. A silver wash-hand basin stands on the table. Along the four walls of the hall are four red velvet chairs. At either end of the hall are three-armed chandeliers with wax candles, also a silver censer and pictures on the doors. From the hall one enters the lord's study; he is sitting at a table and beside him are books, a violin, a lute, a sporting gun, a pistol, sword and dagger, money chest and writing cassette. An English dog stands by the door. A messenger is sitting outside the hall door, a boy is offering him something to drink. From the hall one enters a passage where a youth is playing the lute, beside him a small monkey. The hall and study are hung with handsome tapestries.

'The Manor Farm estate also includes a farmhouse. Here, the family lives in a room immediately to the left as one enters the front door. On the stove, which has a wooden railing around it, are two vinegar jars. Lazy Leonard is lying asleep on the bench. A yarn winder, a spinning wheel and a water vessel are standing on the bench surrounding the stove. A child with a bowl of milk is seated on the table, beside it a loaf of bread. A cat sits on one of the two chairs by the table, and on the floor are a black dog and two hens. A child is riding his hobbyhorse. The grandmother is sitting on the bench and spinning, a grandchild beside her. Next to them is a small folding table. A towel is hanging over a wooden towel holder on the door, and next to this is a washing box, with four country glasses in it; a copper jug is hanging beneath the wash-hand basin. In the chamber, a bedstead for two persons with a half-tester, before the bed a low chest containing the clothes of the farmer's wife, beside it a green chamber pot and a pair of country shoes. Between the windows, in a chest, the farmer's clothes. A child's cot is there as well. On the opposite side, a linen press and beside it another child's cot. From the passage leading to this chamber, another leads to the 'privy chamber' where a maid is relieving herself, with another emptying a pot in the middle of the passage.'

These old records sometimes refer only briefly to what no doubt was a matter of course to the writer, making it difficult for us to understand what exactly he was saying. On the other hand they are so marvellously descriptive that we can get a good impression of what the houses were like. Quoting them in some detail will save us the trouble later on of having to describe in detail the dolls' houses that are still extant and are illustrated with many photographs in this book. The basic layout, furnishing and fittings remained the same right into the nineteenth century, but naturally there are numerous variations in the details and these lend each house its individual character and its own particular charm.

In Johann Hübner's *Curioses und reales Natur-, Kunst-, Berg-, Gewerk- und Handlungslexicon* (Encyclopaedia of Curiosa and Realities in Nature, Art, Mining, Trade and Commerce), the fifth, enlarged edition of which appeared in 1727, fifteen years after the first edition, the entry under *Puppenhaus* (Dolls' or Baby House) reads as follows:[12] '... with everything that is required in a household, for ornament and display as well as for necessity, most agreeably and in part expensively reproduced, deftly arrayed and stowed away in the apartments and rooms, and in the cupboards and chests, containers and presses to be found therein.' In his *Grosses, Vollständiges Universal-Lexicon* (Great Encyclopaedic Dictionary), Johann Heinrich Zedler further adds in 1741: '... For there is probably no trade where the things usually made in full size are not also fashioned in very small models, with the cities of Augsburg and Nuremberg in particular being ahead of others in this respect'[13]. Nothing is said, therefore, of such a dolls' house also being a toy for children.

A Baby House is mentioned in the inventory of the estate left by Johann Christoph von Lemp auf Ebenreuth[14], a well-to-do Nuremberg merchant who died in 1712. His grandfather had come from Eger to the free imperial city as a Protestant exile during the Thirty Years' War. He was raised to noble rank by the Emperor Leopold I, and a son and a daughter of his married into the Nuremberg patriciate. A 'Baby House with all appurtenances' stood in the chamber belonging to the vestibule of Johann Christoph von Lemp's house; its value was put at 25 guilders. It is extremely difficult to estimate the modern money equivalent of such a sum, as we do not know the exact nature or the state of preservation of comparable items. In Lemp's estate, a 'walnut press' (wardrobe with walnut veneer) was valued at 24 guilders, a large varnished press with five doors, three drawers and carved angels' heads, on the other hand, only at ten guilders (probably an older piece of furniture, in any case still seventeenth century), a walnut table, its leaf (top) painted, at as much as 30 guilders, and a writing table stained black, its foot (base) inlaid with crystal (rock crystal) and gold, together with a mirror with green and other false stones, at 50 guilders. The marriage bed carved in walnut which in 1682 had formed part of his wife's dowry and complete with everything had been rated at 200 guilders, was 30 years later considered worth only 110 guilders. One gets the impression that it was the value of the materials that counted and not the workmanship. Most of the materials used for a dolls' house were not expensive – unless of course it was a princely Baby House, like the Munich House – and the Lemp House no doubt was handsomely furnished.

Anna Köferlin's House (1631)

The real 'value' of a Baby House lay in the work done to create it, usually by a large number of skilled craftsmen. Yet this hardly played any role in the actual price put on it. This is very well demonstrated by the 1631 Nuremberg House of Anna Köferlin[15]. We know of its existence only from a woodcut broadsheet. During the middle years of the Thirty Years' War, when times were hard indeed, this Nuremberg woman, childless and clearly not well-to-do, built and furnished a Baby House several stories high, a task calling for considerable personal engagement and persistence, and obviously not intended as a financial investment. Anna Köferlin undoubtedly did not build the house by herself, but merely provided the driving force behind the effort. As to the actual money she spent on it, that probably would not have bought one of the heavy gold chains much prized by nobles as well as commoners everywhere from the sixteenth century onwards; from portraits of that period we know that several of these were often worn, each of a different length. Johann Christoph von Lemp possessed many valuable items of jewellery, among them two gold chains, one estimated at more than 50, the other at more than 35 guilders, and a heavy gold chain worth more than 28 guilders.

On the other hand it has to be remembered that only well-to-do families could afford a Baby House. The House owned by Anna Köferlin, a simple commoner, appears to have been an exception. Baby Houses were normally cherished as private possessions, but she proudly exhibited hers for money. It was thought until now that Anna Köferlin was not married, but the poem on her broadsheet merely states that it had 'not been granted to her to be the mother of children'. In the records of the Nuremberg regional church archives an Anna Köfferle has been traced who had two children, born in 1598 and 1599, both of whom apparently died early, so that this remark may well serve to confirm her identity. This would make her a Hübner by birth, from Neustadt (on the river Saale?) and the daughter-in-law of the cipherer Simon Köferll who died prior to February 1592. In 1596 she married his son Hans (John), probably born in 1574 and presumably a shopkeeper; he died in 1632, his widow in 1647. Thus the broadsheet, in those days the customary form of advertisement, was printed to attract visitors to the Baby House. It shows a woodcut House, and beneath it a poem, in the long-winded style of the period, telling of the aim and purpose of the attraction, a 'Baby House, the like of which was never before seen or made'. The rough doggerel verse starts with the emphatic statement: 'Wherefore man be sensible and sane, born to labour... And moreover if he be young and sound in wind and limb, he shall for nought let any hour pass without work done.' Further on we read: 'A wife is but a weak tool, to direct big works, many a time she will be failing. But when we truly look upon her housework and the great care and trouble she does have with young infants from morn to night, we shall soon find that she can never take her ease.' To Anna Köferlin herself it had 'not been granted to be the mother of children', but she, too, did not want to take her ease: 'But what is there placed before your eyes, prepared without complaint over some years for the young, put together with industry and much effort, to provide instruction for the young, that they, too, shall from their young days become accustomed always to be doing ... Therefore, dear children, look you well at everything, how well it is arranged; it shall be a good lesson to you. So when in time to come you have your own home and God willing your own hearth, you will for all your life put things nicely and properly, as they should be, in your own households. For as you know fine well, as our dear old ones used to say: Where disorder reigns in the home, there it is soon over; disorder is a poor ornament. So look you then at this Baby House, ye babes, inside and out. Look at it and learn well ahead how you shall live in days to come. See how all is arranged, in kitchen, parlour and chamber, and yet is also well adorned. See what great number of chattels a well-arrayed house does need. But at times one may also manage well with little, if one be content. Look all around you, look behind you, look everywhere, how much there has been put on show for you, hundreds of pieces. Of bedding, of handsome presses, of pewter, copper and brass, fitted up in such a way that though small, yet everything may well be put to general use. Every piece, mark you well, one hither, the other thither may be of use, to serve its purpose. There are parlour, chamber, cellar, kitchen, and also the corn-loft. . . . Stringed instruments you find, to while away the time, lutes and violin, to strike up a tune. A flute and a piccolo you will find there as well, to join in the merry-making. And there in a corner you have books standing well arrayed, as in a library, to look at one after the other. An armoury where all manner of armour may be seen, rifles, harness, weapons, rapiers that one might almost be afeared. Cuirasses for man and horse, diverse arms for war, to be beheld and marvelled at, that you may forget to shut your jaw. One also sees there upon the wall many a thing painted, as one may also see the hand of many an artist in parlour, chamber and halls. . . . The height of this house is nine foot; five foot its width, and the depth four feet . . . The cellar always holds a store of all kinds of drink, wine of Istria, malmsey, red and white wines, beer. So that what a company of twelve strong men may want to drink, I can provide enough to have them stagger and reel. In sum, all in proportion, all in a small compass is everywhere made, with care and effort early and late. That if I wish'd to tell of all there is to see in there, this paper would the like be too small, I must confess. But as it only presents to you the outer form, you will be served much better if you come and see how it is arrayed. Thus I have tried in sum to give note of this here. Those who have not seen it, shall still come; to them too it will be shown with good will. I know that their time and trouble will not be in vain.'

The height of the house, approx. 240cm, and its width of 134cm, is no less astonishing than its depth of about 100cm. The façade shows the year, 1631, and the Latin inscriptions PRINCIPIO RESPICE FINEM (In my beginning I consider my end) and SOLI DEO GLORIA (To God alone the glory). The beetle at the bottom left provides an indication that the signature HK stands for a member of the family (German *Käfer* = beetle; Köferlein = *Käferlein* = small beetle), perhaps indeed her husband, Hans Köferlein.

On the ground floor, the main entrance is flanked by columns, with two figures reclining on the gable. Two upper stories rise above it, each with five front windows, the middle one in each case projecting as a bay or oriel of the type popular in Nuremberg from the fourteenth century. Three other windows have small projecting structures in front, up to half their height. The steep roof appears to be tiled and to contain two attic floors, for there are two rows of three dormer windows. The side

of the house also has windows, again with bottle-glass, and the gutter spouts are two animal heads with mouths agape. With all these features, the house appears to have much in common with the Bäumler Family House in the Germanische Nationalmuseum in Nuremberg.

Baby Houses from Nuremberg and at Augsburg

An account from the late seventeenth century referring to a Baby House confirms that it was not a piece for ostentatious display by commoners, but indeed a magnificent cabinet piece, a work of art. The 1671 inventory of the castle at Pottendorf in Lower Austria lists one of the items owned by Count Franz von Nadasdy and kept in his treasury[17] as: 'Cupboard No. 4: a Nuremberg Baby House stained black, divided into 17 rooms, some of them wainscotted. Inside are two mirrors studded with false stones, all kinds of household stuff made of ivory, 52 pieces in all, and others of white and black alabaster, 21 pieces, two flasks of serpentine, 24 pictures and Agnus Dei, partly modelled in wax. Presses and chests, beds, stoves, and everything needed to furnish a household.' Close to the border of Austria's Burgenland, this showpiece of a Nuremberg Baby House stood in the art cabinet of a rich magnate, a man who was being dispossessed and soon afterwards executed.

In 1765, the Augsburg patrician and historian Paul von Stetten the Younger described in his *Erläuterungen der in Kupfer gestochenen Vorstellungen aus der Geschichte der Stadt Augsburg* (Commentary on the Copper Engravings showing Scenes from the History of the City of Augsburg)[18]: 'Concerning the training of maidens, I must make reference to the playthings many of them played with until they were brides, namely the so-called Baby Houses. These contained everything that was needed for house and home, presented in miniature, and some went so far in lavishness that such a plaything came to be worth something like a thousand guilders or more. Yet no young female ever read more than devotional books and the calendar, and even these none too well, nor was any trouble taken to teach them anything apart from their household duties, and their language and mode of expression was no different from the manner of speech of their maids. There were some who knew a little more, but their numbers were very small.'

Paul von Stetten therefore actually refers to toys, but one must consider the extent to which he himself was subject to the views held during his time, in the second half of the eighteenth century. He does add that some Baby Houses cost a thousand guilders or more, so that it cannot be a question of toys as we consider them today, to be handled and manipulated, but 'dolly' or 'puppet' work as it was understood then – items produced in miniature and not for real use, not something distinct in its own right, but rather a miniature edition of something else.

The famous Pomeranian Cabinet, sent to Stettin in 1617, together with the Manor Farm of Philip Hainhofer, might be regarded as such a 'plaything'. With all the valuable items it contained, and its intricate workmanship, it was estimated to be worth at least twenty thousand guilders. A Baby House worth a mere five per cent of that must still have been a magnificent 'art' piece in a middle-class household. The fact that it also contained silver utensils is not surprising if one remembers that during the seventeenth and eighteenth centuries the goldsmiths' trade was flourishing in Augsburg. The Nuremberg Baby House owned at some time by the Kress von Kressenstein patrician family is also said to have contained silver objects before it came to be in the Germanische National-museum, about one hundred years ago[19].

Paul von Stetten puts great emphasis on the fact that in those days the middle-class housewife's whole life was taken up with the household and her own family that were in her care. Her horizons had scarcely widened since the Middle Ages. Women of the upper middle class lived within a narrowly confined sphere at that time, like the farming and artisan population, a sphere not extending beyond their place of residence and its immediate vicinity. House and home were their universe, a well-ordered world, the significance of which it is difficult for us really to apprehend. Fully ordained and complete in itself, everyday domestic life held its own good measure of tasks and duties related to the cycles of the day and of the year and to the different stages of life.

Household and management utensils

Among the incunabula of German literature are a book published in Lübeck in 1492, and another published two years later in Augsburg entitled *wie ein yegklich man haushaben und sein haus egi en soll* (How Every Man Shall Keep and Govern his House). These, and the cookery books called *küchenmaistrey* that have been published in Nuremberg, Augsburg and Mainz since 1485, show that the demand for such instruction in everyday middle-class household affairs was so great that many were issued just a few decades after the invention of printing. A few handwritten patterns for embroidery and woven ribbons, i.e. for women's needle-work, have come down to us from late fifteenth century and early sixteenth century Nuremberg[20]. In 1523, Johann Schönsperger of Augsburg, who also did fabric-printing, published the first book of printed embroidery patterns. In Italy, the first printed pattern book was published in 1527; characteristically this contained lace patterns. In 1593, Johann Coler brought out a large tome, *Oeconomia ruralis et domestica*, later called *Housekeeping book* in short. This gives very detailed instructions on everything relating to the sphere of duties of the master or mistress of the house. New editions continued to appear for 120 years. At the end of the seventeenth century, Johann von Hohberg first published his *Georgica curiosa*, three thick folio volumes illustrated with copper engravings.

Considering the great number of everyday household articles listed in such inventories as have come down to us, very little indeed has actually survived from four, three and even only two hundred years ago. Things became worn out, were used up, or later came to be considered useless and 'old-fashioned' and were thrown away as lumber and old iron. Utensils of pewter, copper and brass, in the inventories often listed merely by weight, were melted down. We do still have some items of furniture, mostly cupboards, chests, tables and chairs; many of these have not been subject to the same wear and tear, especially if they had been items for display which later generations preferred to keep. Of the valuable pieces of goldsmiths' work, only a fraction has survived to this day, but even less is still in existence of implements made of non-precious metals and from wood. Textiles such as cloth covers, cushion covers, curtains, towels, bed and table linen are practically nonexistent in Germany, and the same applies to items of clothing dating back to prior to 1700, where only the occasional original item is still extant. Everyday middle-class eating utensils, jars and baskets, brooms and other domestic implements, those innumerable bits and pieces that are so useful – almost all of these have become lost. Anything we know about them comes largely from contemporary records, inventories and books of housekeeping, letters and documents; or one may see them here and there in engravings, woodcuts and paintings. Some museums and collections do occasionally still have such items. But it is in the large Baby Houses of southern Germany, and particularly those of Nuremberg, that everything has been preserved in its entirety, albeit on a small scale. The Germanische Nationalmuseum has four whole Houses and several rooms of the seventeenth century; others may be found in the Magdeburg museum[21] and in the Victoria and Albert Museum in London, or in its annexe at Bethnal Green[22]. The House kept in the Schlossmuseum in Berlin[23] was lost in 1945. The Bavarian National Museum in Munich[24] has an Augsburg Baby House, and the Basle[25] and Strasbourg[26] museums each have one of local origin. The contents of these seventeenth century Houses may have been added to, or changed to some extent, during the eighteenth and nineteenth centuries, but on the whole they still contain items belonging to the period of their origin and it is to these that they owe their general character.

Like Anna Köferlin's House of 1631, the Nuremberg Dolls' Houses originally had a front façade where one peeped in through small window openings, not the wide glass panes used today. Being – of necessity – designed for display to one side only, these Houses are fundamentally different from 'real' houses. They are not scale models of an original house, but present such a house to be viewed from one side, with the architecture and furnishings designed to that effect.

The oldest of the Nuremberg Houses

The oldest of the Houses on view in the Germanische Nationalmuseum, which is also the longest, does not have a high gabled roof like the others. One has to imagine the sloping roof hidden behind the closed façade at the top, which has five windows. Quite recently, the date 1611 was discovered, in a place not previously noticed on the ground floor. The base is designed as a cellar, with several doors leading to it. On the inside of the door on the right is a painting of a maid, barefoot and with a wooden tub in her arm; she is taking a child, already undressed and carrying a dipper, to the bathroom (which one would therefore imagine to be nearby); both are wearing round 'bath hats'. Another door shows a vaulted passage where a servant, fashionably dressed, with feathers on his hat and wearing a ruff, is polishing some long riding boots. A unique feature is the great hall on the ground floor, its walls partly decorated with pic-

1–13

2

3

1

tures painted on paper, no doubt intended to represent frescoes or tapestries. The artist had taken his design from an engraving by Jan Sadeler the Elder who in turn had taken it, though left and right reversed, from a drawing by Dirck Barendsz (1534–92), but he had made some changes and added to it considerably[27]. A merry company is seated at a table in the garden. In the top right corner of the wall at the back, three women and a youth may be seen having a game of cards, with a maid filling a goblet. As is usual in Nuremberg, the wainscoting only covers the walls to three quarters of their height, leaving room for dishes and ornaments to be arranged on the cornice. The cellar may be reached through a trap door in the plank floor of this hall. The large yard next to the hall has a triple gallery on the right, with gilded balustrades. The upper gallery continues along the back of the yard, where monks and nuns are painted fondling and caressing. The water for the flower gardens comes from a well at the corner of the yard, its sides and high back panel decorated with colourful paintings and ornaments framed in gold. The yard not being an indoor space, its 'ceiling' has been partly decorated with a moon and stars. On the left, a staircase leads to the first floor. Here one finds the kitchen, as in all Nuremberg Baby Houses, whilst in the centre section the stairs continue to the second floor. The walls of the staircase show paintings of maids and of young troopers parading their lances, spears and halberds, and above and beside the doors those of deer, their modelled heads projecting from the wall. The landings have tall doors leading to the kitchen and various rooms. The family living room opposite the kitchen was given new wainscoting, furniture and a white stove in the middle of the eighteenth century. However, the original garlands of flowers painted above the wainscot are still there, as also in the room above, which was given some additional furniture in the early nineteenth century, and in the state-room which is on the second floor right.

Apart from the yard, every room of this House was originally framed on its front-side in a rounded arch supported on balusters, with a balustrade below; the framing has survived almost complete around the staircase, but elsewhere only the half-balusters up the sides remain. The ceilings of the living room and state-room are wainscoted, as usual, apparently, at that time, for in the other Nuremberg Houses these rooms stand out in a similar fashion. The other ceilings are painted, even if only in stripes or squares. The attic floor is also decorated with a pattern of stripes, but to see this one has to open the bolted 'bottle-glass' windows. The house is 241cm high, 195cm in length, and 58–62cm deep.

The Nuremberg Baby House of 1639

The Baby House bearing the date 1639 on its middle dormer probably still looks much the same as it did at the time of its origin. From floor to gable, it measures only 203cm. Its length is 152cm, its depth 50.5–52.5cm. This is only half the depth of the Köferlin House, but in relation to the size of the House this depth appears considerable, making the small rooms in the base into quite long corridors. All but one of these are whitewashed. The one with panelling, probably intended to mark this, the nursery, as distinct from the servants' bedrooms, also has an ornamental painted ceiling, whilst the ceilings of the other rooms only show coloured stripes. The landings on the first and second floor and the room at the top left have particularly handsome painted ceilings, whereas those of the living room and state-room (above the kitchen) are panelled. Those two rooms have wooden flooring; in the others, a patterned design suggests tiled floors. The entrance hall on the ground floor has its floor painted to imitate cobblestones. In the wainscot on the walls, a corner was always left free for the tiled stove. In the room above the living room, the walls have been pasted over with a paper imitating grain of wood (probably a later addition). The

walls of the entrance hall and first landing have been given the appearance of square blocks of sandstone, with the upper cornice of the architectonic door frames continued partly across. The painted wall at the back of the second landing imitates heavy wall hangings. Both landings have not only doors leading to the adjoining rooms, but also bottle-glass windows providing additional light. In the literature, this House is referred to as the Stromer Baby House. But the von Stromer family only owned it from 1862 to 1939, loaning it to the Germanische Nationalmuseum from 1879 on-

wards. Its existence was known in 1825, when Emilie Ernestine Baroness von Haller (d. 1856) acquired it from the estate of Karl von Wölckern[28]. Her eldest daughter Helene Christine married Christoph Gottlieb Friedrich Baron von Stromer in 1847. It appears that this was how the House came to be in the possession of the Stromers. The original owner can no longer be traced. The lion behind the diamond lattice of the oval window above the entrance is not thought to be an armorial beast, and therefore cannot give an indication as to whoever commissioned the House. The

Fig. 3 Jan Sadeler the Elder: Banquet, part of an etched representation of The Last Judgement. The painting in the 1611 Nuremberg Baby House is made after this (see Fig. 13).

fifteen rooms contain more than a thousand small and very small objects. It seems that nothing has been forgotten, from the many beds complete with pillows and covers, their linen decorated with lace and embroidery, the full presses, and coffers, pictures on the walls showing various landscapes and allegorical representations of the virtues, a rocking horse, some small wooden chairs and a walker for the children, games for the grown-ups, all kinds of earthenware, some of it glazed, brass, copper and pewter utensils, right down to the distaff, boards for linen or victuals, a neatly arranged tool box, troughs, vats and wine barrels, and finally the wheelbarrow, a rake and the cattle in the stable. This, by the way, is the only room not connecting with others by way of a door. It has a side door from the outside, on the left of the house, for the use of the lad who is painted on it. Otherwise the House is entered by the portal at the centre of the front. To the left and right of the entrance hall are the wine cellar, a store-room, a shop, also fitted to serve as the merchant's office, the laundry, and three bedrooms for children and servants. In the upper stories, a bed has been placed in the family living room and also in the room above it, the latter probably serving as a bedroom only. Contemporary paintings and engravings also show large and small groups of people eating, playing games or making music in rooms that have

a bed in the corner. And this is indeed how it must have been, and not only in a Baby House where it has not been possible to reproduce the chamber that went with almost every room in the house, not necessarily smaller than that room, and usually facing the yard rather than the street and unheated. In 1712, for example, the marriage bed stood in the 'chamber of the best room' of Johann Christoph von Lemp's house in Nuremberg[29]. It was of carved walnut and had a painted tester and a low chest by the side. This chamber contained two more beds that were somewhat less elaborate, and two large presses. The furniture of the 'best room' consisted of the walnut table with painted top and the magnificent writing table stained black that have already been mentioned, as well as mirrors, *gueridons* (tall, narrow stands for candles, vases or other single items that became fashionable in the late seventeenth century), and silk-covered walnut chairs. In Lemp's 'new house', a bed stood in the 'Grässel room' (the maiden name of Lemp's wife Dorothea Sabina who died in 1701, after 19 years of married life, had been Grässel), this was a wooden bedstead with six yellow silk curtains; others stood in the landscape room, in this case a decorated bed with ribbons and a painted bed; a bed painted blue stood in the blue room, another painted red and yellow in the red and yellow room.

During the Middle Ages, city houses had only narrow street fronts, but extended well back on their plots. They were half-timbered or of stone, and even in those days reached a respectable height, having two or more stories above the ground floor, beneath a steep, gabled roof. The lower part of the house was occupied by 17/ the craftsman's work and store rooms, the 18 merchant's shop, or wholesale dealer's office, also the store rooms for commercial goods and comestibles, barrels of wine and beer, sometimes a pot-room, a wardrobe, the laundry and then the bathroom, and in most cases also a stable. The kitchen with a 28 separate larder was on the first floor. Not far from it, on the other side of the central landing in the Baby Houses, where the 23 stairs were and the 'privy chamber', was the family living room, later also known as the dining room, for there stood the large 54 table where meals were taken together. On the second floor was the parents' bedroom, sometimes a guest room also, and above all the salon or state-room, the most elegantly and richly furnished room in the house. There guests were received and family events celebrated. The *Hauss-Halterin*[30] (house-keeper), published in Nuremberg in 1703, also refers to it as the 'state or audience chamber'. It should perhaps be mentioned at this point that Baby Houses reflected the houses of well-to-do citizens in their layout and furnishings, not those of simple artisans. When the prosperous gentleman came to have his own separate office where he would also house his library, the mistress of the house also had her own lady's cabinet or dressing-room, at least at a later date.

Windows and curtains

During the seventeenth century, window panes were of leaded bottle-glass, allowing only dimmed light to enter the rooms. In 23 the Baby Houses, these are generally only painted. Occasionally a large window encompassed a smaller one of clear glass that could be opened on its own and also per-mitted a clearer view of the world outside. In 1587, Magdalena Baumgartner of Nuremberg wrote to her husband Balthasar[31] that in her opinion twenty 'Batz' was a lot of money for such a peeping window of (white) Venetian glass, and she therefore wanted to wait for the return of the master of the house before deciding on the purchase. Nor was she sure as to the best position for it; placed in the centre window of the room, it would not appear in the middle window of the house when seen from outside. In 1661 and 1662, Georg Friedrich Behaim, too, was asked a not inconsiderable sum for a few 'hollow' (concave) glasses for the windows of his dungeon (a garden house behind the city wall)[32].

As a protection against cold and draughts, and also against strong sunlight, windows were often fitted with wooden shutters on the inside. Window curtains took a very long time to gain general acceptance in Germany. However, in two paintings from the Upper Rhine region representing the Annunciation, one about 1420, the other about 1460, red and green curtains respectively are shown affixed to rings on an iron rod; these could be drawn across the window or even the whole wall[33]. In 1495, when Sebald Schreyer of Nuremberg, who among other things was Church Master at St Sebaldus Church, had his 'front room' in the House at the Preachers newly done up before the feast of St John[34], mention was also made of the irons with rolls, to curtains there and in the upper chamber, that one might draw them across and back; this no doubt refers to window curtains. But generally, if curtains were mentioned in inventories and house-hold books, they usually were bed cur-tains, well into the seventeenth century. It was probably in the bedchamber that win-dow-curtains first came to be more widely used. During the first half of the sixteenth century, window curtains were considered both expensive and unnecessary in Nurem-berg. This is evident from a note made by Kaspar Kress in 1525, that he had given his daughter, married to Joachim Haller in 1522, the loan of a 'green arlass curtain together with two window curtains also made of green arlass and a fine curtain for the door' to furnish the room for her confinement[35]. The 1542 inventory of Paulus Laufenberger of Strasbourg refers to a blue curtain before the windows of the upper chamber, a room that apparently was not a bedroom; the other rooms clearly had no such protection[36]. In 1550, Paulus Behaim of Nuremberg acquired pink and green '*schetter*' (buckram) for curtains in his bedchamber[37], thirteen years later he bought green '*arlass*' (linen stuff) for the same purpose[38]. The estate of Michael Schramaeus, secretary to the Bishop of Strasbourg, included in 1613 three old blue curtains of '*engelsitt*' (a light woollen material) before the windows of the room and the bay, also two of white linen[39]. The inventory of textiles acquired by Count Palatine Johann Friedrich (1587–1619) records 'window curtains of black double taffeta' and 'curtains for windows of sulphur yellow viol crimson red and green mesh' (striped in different colours and with red and green fringe?)[40]. Johann Maximilian zum Jungen of Frankfurt-on-Main paid money for forty yards of blue printed stuff for curtains in 1646, but it is not clear what these were intended for[41].

Floors and walls

Looking at the Nuremberg Baby Houses, 26 it is clear that plank floors were the norm for living and state rooms. In other rooms, the floors usually were of black and red 34 brick, or tiles glazed in white and various colours, arranged in a geometric pattern. In 1562, Paulus Behaim of Nuremberg had 1150 black and red paving-stones laid in two bigger chambers and one small one[42]. Hans Bien's 1625 drawing of the Nurem-4 berg house of the Teutonic Knights shows red and white chequered stone floors as well as plank floors[43]. In the 1703 *Hauss-Halterin* we read of stone floors painted with oilpaint for the landing, and even, as

something very special, of marble floors[44]. Parquet floors only became fashionable during the eighteenth century.

Wainscoting is mentioned in 1495, when Sebald Schreyer of Nuremberg had his 'front room' done up[45]. First, the wooden ceiling and one wall, which were panelled already but had probably become blackened, were planed, then the three other walls were wainscoted to more than half their height, whitewashed above, and painted with green foliage just below the ceiling. Chests were affixed to the wainscot all around – these also served as seats – and 10 furthermore eight small containers that could be locked. A large unlocked kist could be converted, with a chest placed before it, to a lazy-bed. This popular type of day-bed, until well into the seventeenth century forming part of the fixtures in a room, with the wainscot, was something of a precursor of the present-day chaise-longue or couch. The *Hauss-Halterin*[46] provides further detail: '. . . being made up with plenty of bedding and a neat cover on top, with a large pillow, very thick and stiff, placed upright at the head end, either in a white cover edged with a band of beautifully embroidered flowers or with lace, or leather on the underside, and decorated on top with colourful embroidery, all kinds of leaves and flowers, and quite often also the arms of the patron of the house; these beds are only rarely uncovered and used, but serve more for appearance than practical use'. This shows that by 1703 they had largely lost their original function and were merely kept for show, a beautifully arrayed relic of former times.

Sebald Schreyer had thirty-three half-length portraits in the style of Antiquity painted above the wainscot on the walls in 1495[47], with the name and a Latin verse written there to go with each; he had nineteen suspension hooks screwed into the wooden panelling, and further hooks to hold candlesticks. Paulus Behaim bought fifteen 'painted and pasted pictures of heads' (papier mâché heads?) in 1557, 'the ancient emperors'[48], probably copies of

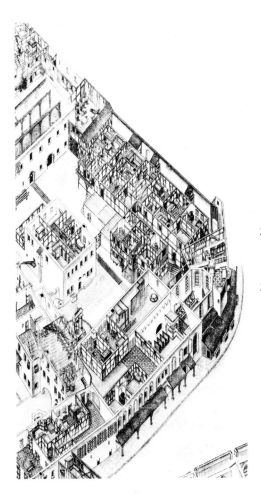

Fig. 4 Hans Bien: Detail from his watercolour showing the first floor of the house of the Teutonic Knights in Nuremberg. Painted in 1625. *Nuremberg, Germanisches Nationalmuseum.*

antique emperors' heads; in the living room – usually referred to simply as 'the room' – eight tall brass candle holders were attached high up round about the following year[49], and in 1563 Behaim finally acquired thirteen *'mendle und frayle'* (small figures of men and women) bossed in black clay (formed and fired), and also horses, to be placed on the cornices[50]. He had had a room on the third floor panelled in 1561, whitewashed above the panelling in 1562, and finally painted at the very top with roses, with the ceiling beams also painted[51]. A hundred years after that, Georg Friedrich Behaim had the four seasons painted on the walls of his garden house at the dungeon, and he also had the 'tales of Rome' – wall paintings depicting the history of ancient Rome restored[52]. The 1622 inventory of Katharina Löffelholz of Nuremberg puts a value of twelve guilders on her '12 old first emperors, large, in plaster'[53]. At the beginning of the eighteenth century, the *Hauss-Halterin*[54] still maintains: 'Usually, paintings are placed on the cornices, with sometimes pyramids, gilded balls, or portrait busts carved in wood or merely cast in plaster, and perhaps also dishes made of porcelain set between them, some leaning against the wall, just as one pleases, and as one's state and purse will permit.' Dishes of that type, not of porcelain, for in Europe that had not been invented by 1703, but of blue-painted Nuremberg faience, alternate with carved and painted vase-like ornaments along the cornices of the large Nuremberg room from the second half of the seventeenth century that may be seen at the Germanische Nationalmuseum, the only one combined with a kitchen below for display not as a Baby House, but as a Nuremberg doll's cabinet. The *Hauss-Halterin*[55] also explains that 'hereabouts' (in Nuremberg) a 'state and audience room' is more usual than the salons to be found elsewhere. According to this book, a salon differed in that the ceiling 'is either painted all the way, or completely covered in stucco-work, or also in such a way that only the central panel, with sometimes one or

32, 35

the other in addition, consist of beautiful paintings, the rest of snowy-white such stucco-work'. From a ceiling of that type, no great chandelier could be suspended, as in a state-room, and light was therefore provided by sconces of silver or brass. But the walls of the salon were not supposed to have wainscoting; they were supposed to be hung with tapestries or covered in fabric, or to be painted to imitate these. The floor should be covered with slabs, or it should be marble, or 'prettily' painted. Instead of the stove, a fireplace was deemed desirable, with andirons, tongs and a poker, the latter with gleaming brass handles.

26

Walls painted with ornaments or arabesques were a cheap alternative to tapestries, silk or velvet wall coverings, or also coloured and embossed leather. Wall coverings of patterned wool and half wool fabrics were also available, later of chintz, and from as early as the sixteenth century onwards flock-hangings; the latter show patterns – in the eighteenth century even whole pictures and scenes – of coloured wool dust on a coarse linen fabric that had been suitably treated. Wallpaper only started its triumphant progress gradually, during the eighteenth century[56].

Stoves and heating

Windows and wainscoting, built-in benches and chests (often called *bankseidel*), as well as suspended and folding tables attached to the walls, formed part of the fixtures of a house and therefore were not normally listed in the inventories of estates, which included the chattels only. For the same reason, these documents do not tell us much about the many different kinds of stove required. These were sometimes quite tremendous structures of green, black or coloured tiles, usually on four or more legs of iron or earthenware. Every room had its stove, but not the chambers, landings or entrance halls. The Nuremberg Baby Houses sometimes have particularly beautifully-made stoves, often real model stoves. In 1625, the Nuremberg house of

26

42

Fig. 5 Augsburg artist, about 1736: Living room. *Nuremberg, Germanisches Nationalmuseum.*

the Teutonic Knights had green tiled stoves, the lower part rectangular, the upper part circular, and also white stoves that were oval below, with a smaller circular structure on top, all on tall iron legs; the high fireplace of the organist's quarters had an architectonic surround[57]. Paulus Behaim had a fireplace in his chamber; in 1548 he bought shovel and tongs for it, and also two iron bars with brass balls, for placing the wood on; the following year he acquired three fire-screens for the fireplace[58] which was used to heat the chamber – for such chambers were normally unheated.

A type of stove that appears to have gained general acceptance during the seventeenth century had a firebox of cast iron plates on legs, with a smaller tiled superstructure[59]. Stoves like these may be seen in the 1736 living room and two studies shown in a series of fourteen pen and wash drawings of interiors from what probably was an Augsburg house[60]. Every one of these stoves is surrounded at its top by drying rods suspended from the ceiling. None of the other rooms, including the large bedroom, have a stove. During the eighteenth century, stoves made entirely of iron came to be widely used. These used less wood, and their arrival had serious consequences for the makers' trade. In Germany, houses were almost exclusively heated with wood and charcoal until the end of the eighteenth century.

Movables

A vivid and often very detailed picture of the movable goods is conveyed by the inventories, share documents and lists of dowries that may be found in great numbers in the archives, and also by the occasional housekeeping books that have survived to give details of daily, weekly and annual expenditure. Many different names were often used for one and the same object in different regions and at different times, and the use and design of such objects tended to vary from region to region; the documents therefore provide much interesting information for the social historian. The rules of orthography did not pertain in those days, and both spelling and the use of names appear to reflect local dialects. This frequently makes it necessary to listen to words over and over again, until their meaning becomes clear. Not only did different dialects change the stem of a word (e.g. 'truhe' or 'truche' for a chest in Franconia, but 'trog' in Alsace), but a number of different names were used for one and the same thing. Thus a press, cupboard or wardrobe would be a 'schap' in northern Germany, 'kalter' or 'behalter' in Franconia, 'kasten' in Bavaria, and 'kensterlin' on the Upper Rhine; another common version is 'schank', not to speak of the names given to special types of cupboards.

Views were very definite as to the proper kind of household goods a home should have during the Middle Ages. A woodcut broadsheet published in Southern Germany about 1470–80[61] shows in 24 small pictures everything considered essential for the dowry of the young couple shown seated at the centre: a wooden bedstead, with tassels at the corners of its large chequered pillow; before the bed, a chamber pot; a pot-shelf with two candlesticks holding one or two candles, three pots, plates, a lidded cup, a pilgrim's flask; barrels, two with their bung-holes closed, the third with a stopcock, also a back-basket holding loaves of bread; a trestle table with a green knobbed glass and a long-necked glass flask; a washing stand with its water container, and next to it a towel on a wooden roller; two cauldrons with movable handles, one of them on three legs, a lidded container, ladle and perforated spoon; a poker, a pot-hook, bellows, a stand and a tripod; broom and sickle; a jar, lidded goblet, beaker and bowl; stable and horse; armour for body, arms and legs; halberd, small sword and sword; boots and spurs; bridle and reins and a hay-fork; sacks; rake and scythe; two ewers, one made of wood staves; a rod with sausages; a basket of eggs and a spice-box; firewood; mirror, comb, scissors, shaving brush, dipper; vegetables and grain; meal-box and storage container; spinning wheel and yarn winder. The verse accompanying the pictures further informs the reader that only a tenth of what is needed could be shown. The sheet bears the name 'hanns paur'.

During the late fifteenth century, Hans Folz, master-singer of Nuremberg, chose house and home as the theme for one of his 'discourses'[62], and 1514 saw the publication, by Grüninger of Strasbourg, of a delightful poem on household goods illustrated with woodcuts and presented as New Year's greetings[63], a long sequence of verses bubbling with a great variety of things. Some objects are actually listed twice, in different contexts, and there is no real order of presentation, with the sequence determined entirely by measure and rhyme. Below, the chattels described in the poem are shown rearranged in groups, putting together related items, to give a clearer idea of the household items then considered necessary.

The list of furniture is as follows: wooden bedstead with a footstool to enable one to climb into the bed, cradle with bench and cradle-band, lazy-bed, food-safe, kitchen cupboard, trestle table, writing table with drawers, counting board, reading desk, wall shelf, book-shelf, chairs, stools, bench, box, chest and case for clothes. 'A wooden roller on the door, with a towel that goes to and fro. By it a water cask with a pretty cock, a brass basin and also a small ewer, for giving water to the masters when at table. And with it also a fine towel, on it many a pretty fringe.'

With the beds, tables, chairs and benches went straw-sack, pillows, sheets, mattress (meaning a quilt), table-cloth and napkins ('fatzilet'), chair cushions and covers, leather cushions and long bolsters. Illumination was provided by a chandelier made from a stag's antlers, brass lamp, lantern, candlesticks ('lyechtstöck'), taper-twist and candles, a screen for a lamp or candle, a candle-snuffer, and for candle-making a rod, warming iron, tray and candle moulds; compasses, hour-glass and astro-

labe are available, and also writing materials: wax tablet, paper, pen, penholder, quills, pen-case stylus, pen-knife, pumice-stone, pounce, sand-box, ruler, and finally the spectacles in their case. The mistress of the house needed a key-cord, scissors, needle holder, pin cloth (pins are stuck into this), a ring to hold small fastening pins, cubit, flat-iron, brush, clothes-brush, yarn winder, reel, weights for the threads when making cords, a weaving frame (gagel-ramen), brake for hemp and flax, hatchel, distaff, spindle rings, spinning wheel, ribbons, a set of brooms, wisp of straw, and a looking glass.

Hammer and tongs were needed, drill, hooks, screws, and turner's and carpenter's bench, a small anvil, compasses and set square, scales and a whetstone, tinder-box and steel, tinder and sulphur sticks, a marking-iron for metal implements.

For the yard, the garden and vineyard, one required spade, rake, line, trimming and carving knives, vintner's knife, wine-keg, a ladder for unloading the wine-barrels, rope and bungs, a supple rod to knock the nuts off the trees in autumn, axe and hatchet, wedges, mallet, flail, yoke, rods, hay-fork and shovel, a fork with hooked tip, dung-cart, a tub for bran.

The laundry was equipped with buckets of wooden staves bound with hoops, tubs and vats, lye-pot and dollies. Added to this there were a ladder, a heating stone, bath-tub, not forgetting for the medicine-chest ear-picks, eye-tweezers, blood-letting cap and bandage, and a bowl to collect the blood, bleeding being a common practice at the time, with a written record kept of this. Other important items were a close-stool, a chamber-pot, and a urinal.

Mouse and rat traps would be needed, a hedgehog skin to frighten off dogs, bird cage and perch, a leather bag ('büttelfas'), a basket for carrying on the back, a basket for wood. A coach, sledge and cart were required for transport.

A great variety of things was needed for the kitchen: a bread-basket with metal mountings, a cabbage basket, a plaited

Fig. 6 Hanns Paur: Woodcut illustration of household goods, from around 1470.
Munich, Staatliche Graphische Sammlung.

basket for smoking cheese and meat, bellows, poker, pan-rester, tripod, pot-hook, hanging iron, fire-pan, iron pans, deep and shallow pots and pans, for eggs for instance, pot-wood and kettle-ring, roasting spit and gridiron, a still, fish-kettle, bowls, pot lids, a pot-bench, well-water basin, water kettle, water tub with lid, boiler for the stove ('*bolle*' or '*gatze*'), pewter and wooden plates, platters, pewter dishes and jugs, a basket for dishes, various glasses, flasks, a mixing jug, an oil jug of green glazed earthenware, a jug of maple wood ('*flader*' = veined or maple wood), another of boxwood, water jug, vinegar jug, maple-wood bowl. 'And bring with you aprons, coarse and clean, and two baskets for dishes that are not too small, containing dishes, plates and also bowls, large and small soup and pap-spoons. Also pots for the pap, bowls, jars and churns wherein to make cheese and butter. Do not forget the spoon basket, wherein are placed many good ladles, that one does eat all kinds of food with.' Two forks (only two, for one did not eat with forks, merely using two-pronged forks for serving – as was still done a hundred years later, for example in the Pomeranian Cabinet and its Manor Farm), banqueting knives, sieve, straining cloth, mortar and pestle, mustard and pepper mill, a stone for grinding spices, spicebox, barberry tub, two large and two small choppers for cabbage and for meat, larding needle, a horn used to stuff sausages, ladle, perforated spoon, grater, funnel, salt-barrel, kitchen board, rolling pin, cake form, jagging-iron, nutcrackers, pot-holders, shave-grass to scour the pewter-ware, and also jugs, bowls, cups of silver and gilded silver. Mention is also made of all kinds of musical instruments, from lute and harp to manichord and trombone and of games, balls and skittles, dice, draught-boards, chess, and games of hazard, and even a carnival mask ('*butzenanlyt*'). Other essentials are a holy-water pot and sprink-ler, prayerbook, rosary, bible, chronicle and book of legends.

This sheer unending multitude may come as a surprise, but the Strasbourg poem of 1514 certainly was no pipe-dream. Its contents were not merely based on Upper Rhine custom, i.e. regional usage, but had general validity and remained applicable for at least another three centuries. It was because it was so utterly right, piece by piece, that the Nuremberg master-singer Hans Sachs wrote a similar poem entitled *Der ganze Hausrat* (The Complete Household Effects) in 1545. A household where everything was the work of one's own hands, and this is how it was not all that long ago, where all was properly made, arranged and kept clean, where in the kitchen everything was prepared, in many different ways, from the raw prod-ucts, such a household had need of a wide variety of implements, some of which we do not even know by name today. People were more or less self-providers in those days, depending largely on their own stores. The 1514 list of household effects was indeed perfectly realistic, witness the numerous inventories of such things pro-duced right into the early nineteenth cen-tury. The great Baby Houses from South-ern Germany may be said to reflect this household reality.

The bed and all that goes with it

In many inventories, the list of valuables – jewellery, money savings, objects of pre-cious metals, of gilded or white silver – was immediately followed by the beds and their contents, shown separately from other furniture. Where inventories are taken room by room and chamber by chamber, the bed or beds are always men-tioned first. The bed was the most impor-tant item of furniture, a basic essential even in the humblest home, be it that of a simple artisan or of a small farmer. The usual wooden bedstead[64] had ropes stretched be-tween the four sides of the frame, either passing directly through the boards form-ing the sides of the bed, or fixed to a frame that was set into the bedstead. Beds might be of plain deal – for the servants, for instance – or of heavy oak or walnut, sometimes decorated with inlays that might be of ebony, even, or other exotic woods, or of ivory; they were veneered and later decorated with marquetry, and mouldings and carving were added for additional ornament; some beds were painted, or completely covered in precious fabrics. From the fifteenth to the eighteenth centuries, many of these beds had a flat or tent-like tester, often covered in painted and later also printed linen or in expensive silk materials. In 1542[65], Paulus Lauffenberger's house in Strasbourg had two such beds with testers supported on four posts in the maid's chamber and in the small chamber on the ground floor; three pictures were painted on the tester of the latter. Two beds, also with testers supported on four posts, on the first floor are called 'welsh', indicating that they were 'modern' pieces, in the style of the Italian Renaissance; one tester had the Angelic Salutation, i.e. the Annunciation, decorating its tester, whilst the other bed had a blue tester, like the one in the maid's chamber, with a matching curtain. Because of their posts, beds like these soon came to be called 'poster-beds' in the Upper Rhine region. The dust cloth, or dust cover, a frame suspended from the ceiling above the bed with cloth cover and cloth hangings, appeared as early as the fifteenth century in that region, and remained popular for a long time. Sometimes the iron rods for the actual bed hangings were also attached to this. In 1590, Christoph Ladislaus Count of Nellenburg[66], provost of the Cathedral at Strasbourg, possessed a dust cloth painted with the Old Testament story of Susanna, above an old veneered bedstead. Johann Theobald Rebstock, bailiff of the episcopal domain of Bernstein in the Alsatian Benfeld, left two bedsteads in 1596[67] that had black dust cloths, one with the arms of Johann Bishop of Strasbourg on the headboard; a third bed had the bishop's arms painted on the dust cloth; two of these beds had truckle-beds to go with them.

In 1580, the estate of the well-to-do Nuremberg patrician Willibald Imhoff[68] included twenty five wooden beds, some with, some without testers, and a number of them with half-testers only. In about 1585, the three sons of Hans Fugger, the great merchant of Augsburg, and Wolf Count of Montfort who shared their student quarters in Padua[69], each had an iron bedstead with a tester of red 'arlas' and curtains of the same linen-material. Two of these beds had a 'truckle' beneath for the servant, a bed that during the day was pushed underneath the young master's. Such truckle or trundle beds were widely used; the term 'rolly' (German *Roller*) or, in the west, *cariol* was used if the bed was fitted with rollers.

Occasionally the lower bed-frame held a number of drawers. These were just as practical as the 'step' before the bed, usually also made of a chest, that was needed to climb into the high beds of that period. In 1612[70], the house of Daniel Prasser (circa 1575–1656), citizen of Wildungen, who was repeatedly elected mayor of that town, contained two large beds with testers, in the chamber at the front and in the one at the back, one with a truckle-bed, and in addition a new bedstead 'with a ceiling to it' (a straight canopy?), a small bed with tester and three drawers in the downstairs room (i.e. in the living room), a simple wooden bedstead in the maid's room, and finally a small child's cot and a cradle with its rocker.

Beds – apart from the simplest ones – would have curtains on two or three sides, depending on whether they stood in a corner of the room or only with the head-end against the wall. In 1594[71], Balthasar Baumgartner of Nuremberg promised his wife Magdalena some blue and yellow silk damask from Lucca, with 'a nice delicate small flower' for a bed as cover, curtains and *'traswerck'* (the short valance, also called a 'garland', draped over the curtain rods). Ten years before this, Magdalena Baumgartner[72] had been most unhappy with a blue material sent to her for curtains. The colour seemed most unusual to

Fig. 7 Woman in child-bed. Woodcut from *Curioser Spiegel*, by Elias Porcelius. Nuremberg, about 1689.

her at that time. In the eyes of this Nuremberg lady, green was the normal colour for curtains; elsewhere, for instance in Alsace, and also at Würzburg or Mainz, other colours were used just as much, and even black, or patterned fabrics in two colours. 'Also the piece that you think to use for curtains is of a most unusual colour and quite unsuitable for curtains, being blue. If it were green . . . If you had first written to tell me the colour, I would have written back to you that it is not suitable.' Frau Baumgartner was also afraid that the material would not wear, as the warp consisted of single threads of silk, making it quite unsuitable for cushion covers or table covers. To her joy and satisfaction she was however able to sell it and now asked for green taffeta instead, the cheaper 'arlas' would be eaten by the moths. She needed six lengths of two and three quarter yards (182cm) each for a bed.

Early in the eighteenth century, bed curtains in yellow and other colours had also come to be used in Nuremberg. In 1712, the estate of Johann Christoph von Lemp[73] included the green curtains from the old marriage bed, white ones with flounces, and yellow and blue, black, rose-coloured and yellow curtains; in 1668, on the other hand, when his grandfather had died, green curtains were in the majority, only one bed had blue and green ones, and one grey and blue striped curtains. Preference was indeed given to green for a very long time in Nuremberg. As taste and preference generally determined the colour of window as well as bed curtains, we may take the example of the 1637 inventory of Maria Löffelholz, née Sitzinger[74] and note that most of the curtains listed in it were green or striped in green, though there were three red and green wool curtains from Arras, red satin hangings, and a curtain of blue stuff. Johann Hieronymus Ölhafen von Schöllenbach had curtains of half-woollen material in 1675[75] that were green on yellow with yellow and green fringes, just as Katharina Löffelholz née Welser[76] had numerous curtains in green or at most

striped in green and yellow in 1622, plus white embroidered ones for one bed.

A straw-sack lay on the ropes of the bed, and then an under-featherbed; this was covered with a linen sheet. The covers consisted of a top sheet, also of linen, and the bed-cover, also called the 'matratze' – a lined quilt, a fur cover, or a featherbed. Like the featherbed, the numerous bolsters and pillows (for the head, shoulders, belly or feet) had covers of ticking or twill (coarse linen woven in diagonal ribs), fustian (cotton twill, less often a cotton mixture), or 'kolsch'. The latter, also called 'golsch' or even 'kölnisch' (Cologne), was popular from late Mediaeval times onwards; originally a coarse linen fabric striped or chequered in blue, this later had 'in a more recent manner, flowers, foliage and all kinds of ornaments most artfully woven in'[77]. It should certainly not be confused with good Cologne linen. In 1598, Johann Theobald Rebstock of Benfeld in Alsace[78] left bedlinen, partly marked with ink, partly embroidered with two kinds of crosses.

The *Hauss-Halterin* gives the following details: 'Beds are not everywhere made up in the same way; in most places, only a little straw is spread on the rope base, covered with a mattress or a cover filled with wadding, cotton or shorn wool and sewn up, and this in turn covered with a sheet; beneath the head is placed a bolster or head-pillow, and as a coverlet another mattress is spread, with a sheet that folds over it.' In the early eighteenth century, therefore, a mattress had in many places taken the place of the straw-sack, though in some places, and not only in the free imperial town of Nuremberg, this was only to gain acceptance gradually, for the better beds. The *Hauss-Halterin* continues: 'Yet here in Nuremberg, and in most places in the German lands, the straw is properly, and that very firmly, tacked together, put into one or two sacks of thick twill or blue and white 'Kollnish' made to fit the length and width of the bed, and placed on the base of the bedstead; one or perhaps two good well-filled under-beds are put on top, with a head and a foot bolster leaning at an angle, whereupon a sheet is spread over it, in such a way that the foot bolster lies underneath, the head bolster on top of it, the head-pillows are stood nice and tall, and the upper bed – some tack a folded-over sheet on it – placed on top.'

Women took a particular pride in their linen and made sure their daughters had a good supply of it for their dowries. Bed-linen of various kinds and qualities had to be provided in some quantity. The best pieces were intended for the marriage and guest beds. In 1580, the inventory of Willibald Imhoff's estate[79] lists the following among the bedlinen: two cotton cambric covers for top quilts, with lace borders, one of linen cambric, one of cotton with punched borders (open-work?), two Lyonnese (linen from Lyons), one St Gallen ticking-cover, one chequered, three pillow-cases with gold braid, eleven with punched borders, four with knitted work, eight with black lace, eight chequered, also punched and laced (slips did not have buttons, or slide fasteners as today, but were laced up one side, as may be seen from some excellent examples in the Baby Houses), 34 slips for belly pillows, two pairs of fine sheets with borders, numerous other sheets, simple ones but always listed in pairs, three pairs of cot sheets, and 29 sheets for servants. Different qualities of linen came from Augsburg, Ulm, Constance, St Gallen, Hesse, Cologne, Westphalia, Silesia, Saxony, and finally two types that were valued highly – from Lyons and from the Netherlands (Flanders). The material might be patterned, either in the same or in another colour, striped, chequered or with borders. Great popularity attached to 'eyed' (diaper) fabrics, i.e. those with a diamond pattern woven in that looked like eyes, either in the same or in a second colour. Some slips were embroidered in white, red or other bright colours, others had coloured or gold borders, and some finally had inset bands of lace or were lace-edged.

Elegant beds would have a cover ('serge') spread over them by day, or a bed-rug, often of silk or wool, in one colour or striped, frequently embroidered, and sometimes lined with buckram. Blue, green or red silk damasks were also used, usually with golden flowers, or block-printed linen. Turkish covers of velvet or silk were lined with wool or cotton. At Schloss Hohenbarr, property of the Bishop of Strasbourg, beds were at the end of the sixteenth century[80] covered among other things with a white 'Catalonian' blanket – a wool cloth from Catalonia of the type then very popular in Western Europe –, a red 'sattlisch' cover (probably meaning 'sattinisch', i.e. indicating satin) lined with red cloth, a black and a white 'tufty' one (with tufts), a blanket of black 'camlet', one of black arras (two woollen fabrics), both with an ash-coloured lining, one red and white, and one green and yellow flowered blanket, a brown flowered satin cover lined with ash-coloured fustian, a white quilted rug, and finally also black and white horse-hair rugs. Where covers are not mentioned specifically in conjunction with a bed, it is usually impossible to say if they were intended for a bed or a table. Special attention appears to have been given to the decoration of the lazy-bed cover; woven tapestry fabrics were popular for this, especially during the sixteenth century. The tester bed of Wennemar von Bodelschwingh[81], a prebendary at Mainz who died in 1605, had a step-up and a truckle-bed and also red and white striped curtains; in addition to the under-bed, the big bolster and three pillows, there was also an old carpet which undoubtedly served as a cover.

In 1701, Dorothea Sabina Lemp[82], wife of Johann Christoph von Lemp of Nuremberg, left a walnut tent-bed with green cloth-tent, curtains and hangings of the same material with green bobbin-lace, and with brass screw and pull in green and white (the tasseled rope used to open and close the curtains and to fix them). The bed had been part of her dowry in 1682. She also left a painted bed 'in the French style' with gilded knobs, covered in red and white woollen material and with bunches of red and white feathers, also six curtains and a valance in these colours, with red and white woollen fringes; it contained two mattresses in blue and white (actual mattresses, as we know them today, instead of a straw-sack, 'in the French manner' meaning that the straw-sack had been replaced with a mattress). On the mattresses lay a large 'ticken' under-bed, a bolster 'the same', both in blue and white damask slips, a large head bolster of fustian, four head-pillows, all trimmed with red taffeta, a large fustian coverlet, two small untrimmed pillows, and two linen slips. The bed, considered to be in the latest fashion, was valued at 150 guilders. Frau Lemp also had a red, embroidered bed-cover with a blue taffeta centre panel and borders in red taffeta, and another of green satin – both valued at 30 guilders each –, one of flesh-coloured, embroidered taffeta (seven guilders), one with its centre patterned in green and yellow and with carmine red borders and yellow fringes (five guilders).

Tables and table-cloths

The *Hauss-Halterin*[83] demands at least two tables for the living room, a dining table which should face the door or stand in the centre of the room, and a work table, for sewing, ironing and the like; also if possible small 'hanging tables', folding tables on the wall. Depending on their intended use, tables might be made from pine, maple, walnut and other more or less precious woods. In 1580, Willibald Imhoff[84] left five maple tables, one of them with numerous compartments, one that could be made round or square (there were fourteen chairs to go with it, so that it must have been of some size), a table with drawers that had a '*thurn*' (= *thurm*, i.e. tower – a board game) painted on it, and also tables of maple, walnut, pear and deal, a table 'both long and wide', two that 'closed up' (probably folding or draw-tables), one 'up-going' one (the top would go up), a writing table with fifteen drawers, finally also a nursery table and two with marble tops, probably framed in wood. There used to be tables with tops of framed slate or of Solnhofen slabs, usually with etched decorations, inscriptions, and indeed song lyrics with the music for all four voices. Simple tables had a plain top resting on a trestle consisting of crossed stands that were only partly given further bracing. Most of the tables in the prince's house at Tenneberg in Saxony in 1637[85] must have been like that; the dining room had two long tables and also one of ash with 'twisted' columns, i.e. legs shaped as twisted columns; a 'small hanging table' is also listed, two tables with drawers, two tables of ash with twisted trestle and one with twisted x-frame stands. Wooden table tops were sometimes painted or ornamentally inlaid with a great variety of fine pictures. The term 'writing table' was until some time in the seventeenth century used for a table with a large drawer and numerous pigeonholes to hold papers, letters and writing utensils. For reading and writing, both scholars and merchants placed a small desk on the flat table top. Both table and desk were often covered with green baize, sometimes also with brown; later, green baize was widely used on conference tables, and there is a saying in Germany today, that some issues cannot be resolved 'around the green table'.

Table tops sometimes served as game boards as well, with a design such as the 'tower' painted onto or carved into the table top. Thus Hans Sachs[86] said: '. . . a game one also knows, called the Tower'. In *ein christlich und nützlich spiel* (a Christian and Useful Game), Johannes Römoldt described it in more detail in 1564[87]: '. . . let us play one and thirty, otherwise called the small tower. Well known everywhere today. Yes, this game I like fine well. The one who deals the cards now cuts. For nought must it be there for money, ere we begin to play'. This early form of the game of *Poch* (poke) was played with cards.

Apart from the painted 'tower' in Willibald Imhoff's estate (1580), a table with a carved 'tower' was also referred to as being in the large room of the Würzburg prebendary Paulus Baron of Schwarzenberg's house in 1557[88], and in Mainz, prebendary Wennemar von Bodelschwingh owned an old tablecloth with a 'tower' in 1605[89]. The same cleric also had an old, long 'ball-shooting' (table), covered in grey cloth, a kind of billiards, no doubt the same game as that recorded in 1712 in Nuremberg, in the house of Johann Christoph von Lemp[90] – a 'drugget' table with cues and balls in the servants' room.

Most tables would have been quite plain, for they were normally covered with a table carpet hanging down the sides, or with a table-cover, often with colourful embroidery showing arms, flowers or 'histories', very similar to the bed covers and if required matching these in colour and design. Here, for example are the most valuable of Willibald Imhoff's (1580)[91] table-covers: a sky-blue damask cover, trimmed with velvet all around (10 guilders), a silk cover embroidered in various colours (24 guilders), a woollen cover embroidered with 'biblical figures' (24 guilders), an embroidered cover of shot-taffety with cotton lining (16 guilders), a large Turkish table-carpet (6 guilders), two Turkish carpets over a long table (28 and 10 guilders respectively); these were probably hand-knotted Turkish carpets, very popular from the early sixteenth century, and not only with the rich burghers of Nuremberg. In Nuremberg as in Alsace, tapestries also served as table-covers. In 1573[92], Hieronymus Imhoff left a Netherlandish table carpet bearing his own and his wife's arms (8 guilders), a second Netherlandish carpet in 'various colours' (3 guilders), and a yellow table carpet flowered in red (5 guilders). In 1582, the note indicating the share of Sabina Behaim, daughter of Paulus Behaim and Magdalena Römer of Nuremberg[93], mentions a striped table cover of 'arlas' (linen-stuff) and a Milan table cover, both reckoned very low in value. A printed Turkish cover, a Turkish carpet and a Spanish blanket are also listed, but it is not clear what these were intended for. Forty years later, in 1622, a share note for the same lady, after the death of her husband Wilhelm Kress, records a table cover with borders and drawn-work in gold thread for four guilders, and also a yellow silk cloth with small green stars (12 guilders), a white Turkey carpet with gold-coloured fringes (7 guilders), and a carpet with black and green roses (4 guilders). In the documents relating to Maria Löffelholz née Sitzinger (d. 1637), it is often possible to determine exactly which items originally formed part of her dowry and see how they became worth less with use in the course of time[94]. Among the covers she possessed, for example, were a large white Turkish one, another of damask that was red and white with a green buckram lining, a white one with embroidery, and one of brown taffeta, also embroidered, one of red silk, scaly patterned and lined with green buckram, one of white, striped cotton with white linen lining, a valuable one with martens' tails, three Persian carpets, one of them coarser with brown lining, four Turkish carpets, one of them in yellow and red with blue borders (probably the type called a Lotto rug, the border with a blue ground), and also a number of older or very plain pieces, each valued at about one guilder only. Regrettably, apart from a few knotted oriental carpets, none of these covers have come down to us, and the few details given in the documents do not really convey much of an impression as to their nature and appearance.

Table and other household linen

The household store of tablelinen, of tablecloths and napkins, would be just as large as the stocks of bedlinen. Linen was either woven at home or the spun yarn taken to a weaver. Any additional material needed would be obtained from the cloth-merchant, with the more well-to-do also going to the Frankfurt Fair. In 1548, the Nuremberg patrician Paulus Behaim[95] bought there three and a half yards of 'damask-work' for a tablecloth with the emperor's arms woven into it, plus fifteen yards for '*fatscheunen*' (napkins), priced at four yards for a guilder, probably because the width of the material was less, whereas a yard of material for the tablecloth cost a whole guilder. This probably was Flanders linen damask, a fabric much esteemed in Southern Germany even before 1500[96]. It was also imported during the second half of the sixteenth century, witness the one or other of the few items that have survived in the possession of certain families, embroidered with the initials of the owner, and sometimes also the year. It seems very probable that linen damask was also made at Augsburg at that time. A cloth 120cm wide with the year 1556 woven into it that was the property of the Augsburg patrician Paul Herwarth and bore his own arms and those of his wife, Magdalena née Welser (in private possession, in the Tyrol), however, was probably not an Augsburg product, but the large tablecloth with the eucharist, the washing of the feet, crucifixion and resurrection and the year 1634 formerly belonging to the Augsburg merchant's family of the Oesterreicher that is now in the Germanische Nationalmuseum. The Augsburg manufacture probably developed from the linen weaving trade existing there since the late Middle Ages, producing towels and tablecloths with coloured bands of ornaments[97]. Two strips of linen-damask were sewn together to give the width required for the 1634 cloth. This was the usual method; a refinement consisted in stitching an embroidered list (strip) down the middle, often in needle-point or net-work. One such damask table-cloth made up of two lengths and also having a 'tongue' (narrow lace edging) at the top and bottom, was in 1597 left by Doctor Andreas Waldner, intendant of the orphanage at Strasbourg[98], who also possessed fifteen dozen napkins with ribs and folded herring-bone (herring-bone pattern between plain longitudinal stripes), a dozen tablecloths with ribs, again with an embroidered list and with 'tongues', two dozen damask napkins, one with lace (wide lace borders), the other with tongues, both with embroidered 'lists' (here possibly hemstitch-borders), finally also two dozen linen napkins with different patterns woven into them, patterns referred to as 'field flower', 'sugar pea' and 'acorn'.

The Bodeck family of Frankfurt, (there were six members in 1665[99]) had three dozen tablecloths, twenty-five dozen napkins, most of them patterned i.e. in patterned damask, all in use. The patterns mentioned in the inventory are: the small grass flower, the wreath of roses, the large rose model, the lavender, the blanched rose, the large flower model, the 'goose-eyed'- and the 'buffi'-model. The names seem very descriptive, as do those used elsewhere – the filled wreath of roses, the rose-cross, the barleycorn – yet as only little of the material has been preserved we are not really in a position to get a clear idea of the different designs. The Leonic (Lyonnese) model appears to have been popular for a long time in Nuremberg, also the triple, double and single barleycorn, and a Netherlandish model.

In 1580[100], thirty-eight dozen napkins were to be found in the Nuremberg house of the well-to-do Willibald Imhoff, though they differed considerably in quality. The best were rated worth half a guilder each. There also were fourteen '*umleg*' (drapes), long narrow pieces of cloth that were attached to the edges of the table where they hung in pleats. Because of the folds in which they fell, these were frequently referred to as '*wasserumleg*' (water drapes) in Nuremberg. Round tablecloths called '*schibentücher*' (disk cloths) were also used at that time.

Apart from table-linen, towels also represented an indispensable item. Long towels, often decorated with woven or embroidered 'lists' (bands) and with lace edges at the bottom, were from Mediaeval times hung up next to the narrow washstand, usually on a roller. Simpler towels were used in the kitchen, like those bought in Hesse in 1642[101] by Johann Maximilian zum Jungen of Frankfurt on Main, with twenty yards costing merely one guilder and six kreutzer. The 1573 inventory of the estate of Paulus Hortulanus, dean of St Peter's at Strasbourg[102], lists among other things four kitchen towels. Even the three young Fugger gentlemen and Count Montfort, when students at Padua in about 1585, had not only twelve assorted table-cloths, 112 napkins, eighteen towels and six 'umblauf' drapes, but also eight kitchen towels[103].

Apart from cut-up linen, in use as bed, table, household and kitchen linen and of course for body-linen, every household that thought anything of itself, and could somehow afford it, did of course also have as great as possible a store of uncut linen stock. In 1712, Johann Christoph von Lemp[104] left a total of 1810 yards of all kinds of cloth: pure (i.e. flax) linen, modelled table linen, also blue and white modelled, blue and white 'Kollnisoh', 'fatscheinlein stuff' (for napkins), white 'diapered' stuff, ticking, white and blue striped, white bed fustian; added to this there was Dutch linen, flowered cotton linen (cotton in tabby weaving), muslin, lawn (specially fine), Ulm linen, Linz linen, damask, flaxen sheeting, clear (smooth) flaxen cloth. This may be compared with the linen stocked in 1601 at Hardwick Hall in Derbyshire, the great English country house of Elizabeth Talbot, the Countess of Shrewsbury[105]. The household goods of this great house have been largely preserved, impressive evidence of the household goods of an Elizabethan country seat. Apart from the linen, everything there is so sumptuous and valuable in both materials and workmanship that we cannot compare with it the commoner's household we are interested in. But where linen was concerned, it was not so much the material that represented wealth, but just the sheer quantity of it. There were linen damasks, diapered linen and plain linen in all kinds of

lengths and widths for tablecloths, towels, napkins and to cover the cupboard, also pieces of fine linen from Cambrai, from Holland, not to mention the pillow-covers and cloths richly embroidered in coloured and black silks or with gold, and decorated with net-work or openwork, usually also trimmed with gold and silver lace and with similar tassels at the corners.

For a long time, the textile goods in a household were considered at least equal in importance to the furniture. With many of the textiles in constant if not daily use and therefore subject to wear, considerable stocks were needed, including those of uncut materials. Unfortunately little has come down to us, except in England where there have been no wars in recent centuries to destroy what was not worn away by use. In the Nuremberg Baby Houses, however, the large presses are still full of cup-up linen, including handsomely decorated items of body-linen for man, woman and child, and rolls of uncut linen of all kinds, and we are able to admire the woven designs then popular, albeit without being able to put the contemporary name to each.

Chairs, stools, benches and seats

Tables and certainly always dining tables and the large banqueting tables were accompanied by chairs, stools, benches and finally armchairs. In 1605, Prebendary Wennemar von Bodelschwingh at Mainz[106] possessed twelve green (painted) 'skabellen' (stools with back rests). In the portrait which Hans Holbein the Younger painted in 1532[107] of Georg Gisze, a merchant born in Danzig and living in London, the whole of the wood-panelling on the wall behind the merchant, with the fillets of wood and shelves fixed to it, is green, a colour highly esteemed at that time; it was the preferred colour for chairs and seats right into the seventeenth century. The 1593 Welcome Book of the Nuremberg patrician Jobst Tetzel[108] shows a room with stone flags, wainscoting to two thirds of the height of

Fig. 8 A round table in the house of the Nuremberg patrician Jobst Tetzel. Painted in 1593, in the Welcome Book of Kirchsittenbach.
Nuremberg, Germanisches Nationalmuseum.

the room, with goblets and dishes placed on the cornice and a bench running all the way round, and also four bottle-glass windows. A festive party is gathered, sitting on green stools around the round table covered with a white cloth on which wooden platters, knives, glasses, goblets and at the centre a dish of fruit have been placed. On the painted lid dated 1619 – the only part still extant – of a spinet formerly owned by Lukas Friedrich Behaim[109] Johann Staden is sitting at a spinet playing the thoroughbass; his chair is similar to the one just mentioned, but its back, like the sides of the stand, is beautifully worked. In Haus Tenneberg in Saxony, a prince's house, but very simple nevertheless during the Thirty Years' War in Germany, the banqueting room contained two long tables and two tables in 1637[110], and besides, nineteen small benches with backs and eight long benches without backs; there were four benches painted green in the Duchess' room. The 1580 inventory of Willibald Imhoff[111] refers to a three-legged chair with 'rails' – this was a back made of rundles, a variation on the chairs called 'skabellen' on the Upper Rhine. In the album of Anton Weihenmayer, mayor of Lauingen, painted by David Brentel in 1586, a lady playing the virginal is seated on just such a chair, its back gently rounded; the book is now at the Germanisches Nationalmuseum[112]. In the engraving entitled *Tischzucht* (table manners), by Conrad Meyer of Zurich in 1645[112], the grandparents are seated in armchairs at one end of the table; the chair-backs consist of two wide strips of leather fixed to the wood with brass nails. The children have been provided with stools decorated with carving; these, and the window seat fitted with a drawer, have thick cushions. In the January tapestry of the series of the twelve months made for the court at Munich in about 1613, after designs by Peter Candid[114], there are four chairs that clearly show the square legs, tall, square uprights for the back, and curved arm-rests, with the seat and back covered in a heavy red

silk fabric; the edges of the fabric at the back are decorated with fringed braid, those of the seat with lambrequins, thick tassels and bobbles; the seats are not upholstered, thick cushions have been placed upon them. Seats, and later also back and armrests, only came to be upholstered in the early seventeenth century; prior to that, loose cushions were always used. This does not mean that the simpler kinds of seats, wooden stools, frequently embellished with painted or carved decorations, went out of use; on the contrary, these were still widely used in the country right into the nineteenth century.

From Medieval times, bench and chair cushions were filled with cotton, wool or straw, and their corners frequently decorated with small or large tassels or bobbles, the latter sometimes called 'acorns'. In 1613, Michael Schramaeus, the bishop's secretary at Strasbourg[115], had six printed green velvet cushions (the simpler type of velvet, usually cotton, with a pattern impressed) with red leather lining, a cushion-sheet with cross-stitch, a cushion with cross-stitch and 'pomegranate' (did it have a pomegranate embroidered in cross-stitch, or was the fabric on the underside patterned with pomegranates?), three 'little cushions' with diverse sheets in '*letzen*' stitch (chain stitch), another with a virgin and the unicorn in cross-stitch, three different 'small bench cushions', flock-filled and with cross-stitch and chain stitch, a cushion covered in yellow silk patterned in green, lined with leather, and finally a small long cushion embroidered in chain stitch. In 1597, Andreas Waldner, intendant of the orphanage at Strasbourg[116], left a total of 24 cushions, embroidered or in '*heidnisch-werk*', the term used on the Upper Rhine for tapestry work, usually with pictures such as the fountain of life, the woman of Canaan, the virgin and the unicorn, Joseph, a virgin with a coat of arms, a woman spinning, Abraham and Isaac, flowers, a garland with a unicorn; three cushion sheets were 'Turkish work' (perhaps knotted in coloured wools, like

68

9

10

Fig. 9 David Brentel: Lady playing virginal. Painting in Anton Weihenmayer's album, 1586. *Nuremberg, Germanisches Nationalmuseum.*

Turkish carpets). At Hardwick Hall, the great house in Derbyshire, the number of cushions, large and small, short and long, was almost too great to be counted in 1601[117].

As the seats and rests of chairs came to be upholstered in the course of the seventeenth century, the number of cushions required declined. However, Georg Friedrich Behaim bought twelve striped seat cushions in 1662[118], no doubt for a dozen chairs or stools. In 1668[119], Andreas Lemp, a well-to-do Nuremberg merchant, left 31 seat cushions, seventeen covers for cushions and bolsters, some embroidered in tapestry yarn (wool), and finally also fourteen window cushions, used to keep out draughts during the cold weather.

Cupboards of all kinds

Mention must be made of the cupboards, large and small, wide and narrow, tall and low. In Medieval times, garments used to be laid flat in presses and chests, but as early as 1498, the inventory of the property of the Strasbourg citizen Heinrich Martin[120] whose estate had been confiscated at the behest of the emperor Maximilian, contained the information that garments could be hung in the press that stood in the large chamber ('ein gewandkensterlin zü hangenden kleydern'). Not very long ago, it proved necessary to change the supposition generally held until then, that the large clothes and linen presses had developed from two chests placed one upon the other[121]. Single-storey presses existed as early as the thirteenth century, their development running parallel to that of two-storey ones which never have been two chests placed one on top of the other. The series already mentioned of pen-and-wash drawings of an Augsburg house shows a large two-storey cupboard with two strong iron handles at the side as late as 1736[122], but that is no indication that these were formerly chests, with the cupboard developed from them; they were merely practical aids to trans-

port. Cupboards and presses were always constructed in such a way that they could be taken apart in sections and put together again. The cupboard shown in the drawing is so tall that the maid needs a three-rise step to be able to put the stack of laundry onto an upper shelf. In the background, another cupboard, also crowned with a low gable, stands against the same wall, and this appears to be single-storey, like the flat-topped one on the opposite wall.

According to the *Hauss-Halterin*[123], the garments were hung on iron or wooden 'screws' in the press, and similar 'screws' – often also of brass – might be fixed to the walls as coat-hooks. For heavy cloaks, the back board of the press should have special 'cloak-woods' (the precursors of coat-hangers); the cloaks were hung over these and if possible also protected with a dust-cloth. For the wide ladies' skirts, 'round sticks' were used, 'with hoops tied around them, narrower at the top and getting wider and wider towards the bottom, that are hung from a screw at the top (of the press) and one or more skirts placed upon them, in which manner they most beautifully keep their pleats uncrippled'. In 1599, Margaretha Röttel, wife of the Strasbourg book-printer Theodorius Rihel[124], left a 'cloak-hang' (a coat-stand?) and two wooden 'veil globes', coif-blocks of the type used until the early nineteenth century, carved from wood and painted, of Frankfurt faience, and even of pottery.

Space does not permit us to consider in detail the wide variety of spacious cupboards and presses, often richly ornamented with metal furnishings, moulding, flaming and other fillets, carving, veneer, marquetry, painted decorations, fixed cut-out ornaments and the like, and smooth, fluted and twisted columns, to store clothes and linen. They showed considerable regional differences. Examples of the type used in Southern Germany may be seen in the Nuremberg Baby Houses, and of those from the Netherlands in the more distinguished Dutch Houses.

Until the seventeenth century, an essen-

Fig. 10 Conrad Meyer: *Tischzucht* (table manners). Engraving, 1645.

Fig. 11 Augsburg artist, about 1736: Room with Cupboards.
Nuremberg, Germanisches Nationalmuseum.

tial item of furniture in Southern Germany was the tall, narrow wash-stand, the Alsatian 'giesfaskensterlin' (water cask cupboard), with its water vessel, often in the shape of an acorn or a dolphin, and hand-basin, usually pewter, in the middle section, and locked cupboards for washing utensils above and below. In the Nuremberg Baby Houses these are placed close to the curtained bed.

Low cupboards, as well as small ones hung on the walls, were used to store letters and papers, writing utensils, glasses and the like. In 1637, the office in the prince's house at Tenneberg in Saxony[125] contained a locked and latticed cupboard with six drawers, and the old office two locked and latticed document cupboards and a cupboard with fourteen locked drawers, probably to store records and documents. It is worth mentioning that in 1637 Maria Löffelholz, née Sitzinger, of Nuremberg[126] left a tall painted book-cupboard with two doors, valued at three guilders.

The Upper Rhine 'trisur' (dresser' cupboard) pyramidically constructed and often covered with clothes, is the precursor of the sideboard. A number of them have been described for the Munich Baby House. In 1597, Andreas Waldner, intendant of the orphanage at Strasbourg[127], owned two 'tresurkensterlin', one veneered and with two drawers, the other with two doors. The latter, probably covered with the 'gebildt' (patterned) 'tresurtuch' (cloth) with ribbons and knotted fringes, was used to store all kinds of 'buppenwerk' (doll's things); these could have been toys, but more likely were trifles such as 'Nuremberg knickknacks'. The 1622 share note of Sabina Kress, née Behaim of Nuremberg[128], after the death of her husband, lists the following 'dockenwerk' ('toys'): '1 fine Jesus boy' for three guilders, '1 ordinary Jesus child' with the Römer arms (the mother's maiden name had been Römer), '1 crying babe' and '1 Schembart' (mask for the Schembart procession at Nuremberg). The Munich tapestry for January dated about

1613[129] shows a cupboard draped in silk to the right of the fireplace, with bowls and other vessels set on its shelves. Before it stands a manservant, a long napkin over his shoulder, who is having some wine poured into a shallow cup. Several of the cupboards in the Nuremberg Baby Houses consist of a low cupboard with a door, sometimes also with a drawer at the base, and a smaller superstructure of two or three levels, with a shallow drawer in each.

Chests and boxes

As in the case of presses and cupboards, it is not possible to go into detail about the many chests, coffers and boxes made from wood, with iron furnishings or wholly of iron, often with several locks or padlocks and ingenious tumblers. These one also finds in the Southern German Baby Houses, as well as the trunks that were the precursors of our suitcases. Before leaving for Osnabrück in April 1646, for the negotiations leading to the Westphalian Peace Treaty, Johann Maximilian zum Jungen, mayor of Frankfurt[130], had two wooden trunks made. In 1590, Christoph Ladislaus Count of Nellenberg, provost of Strasbourg Cathedral[131], had his arms put on one of his two travel chests. He also possessed two 'gutschentröglein' (coach chests) made to measure for his travelling coach. In the 'kellerschopff' (basement) of the 'honourable well-born gentleman' stood a covered open-framed travel wagon, its basket woven of willow-wands, a coach covered in leather fully equipped with everything, including 'its travel chests', and a travelling coach with black covers. Hans Bien's drawing of the house of the Teutonic Knights at Nuremberg (1625)[132] shows a coach in the coach house with a long shaft, its black roof lined in green. In 1712 Johann Christoph von Lemp[133] owned a sleigh with double 'Geleit' (set of bells?), bunches of feathers and other accessories; this was valued at 75 guilders, so that his Baby

House, at 25 guilders, must have been a fairly modest one after all.

As may be seen in the oldest Nuremberg Baby House still extant – the one with the year 1611 written in a hidden place – hunting trophies decorated mainly the corridors and landings of houses. Stag's antlers ('hirschgewichte') were popularly placed on carved or modelled animal heads emerging from the wall. In the prince's house at Tenneberg in Saxony[134], three stag's heads were in the office, in 1637, 28 in the passage outside the banqueting hall, nine in the chamber next to it, five in what was called the 'bear' room, and another five in the hall.

Lighting

Antlers, or rather the cast beams, could also be used to make a chandelier for the living room. Albrecht Dürer designed the large gilded chandelier made by Veit Stoss from two reindeer beams which the patrician Anton II Tucher donated for the town hall at Nuremberg and which is now in the Germanisches Nationalmuseum[135]. In 1557, the estate of Paulus Baron of Schwarzenberg, and prebendary at Würzburg[136], included a chandelier for six candles in the large room of his house, made from a set of antlers, with a Judith, a figure of the Old Testament heroine, supporting the family arms.

As in the Baby Houses, many of the chandeliers hanging from the centre of the ceiling were cast in brass. Illumination was also provided by sconces on the walls and by candlesticks holding one, two, three or more candles on the table, usually of wood or brass, but also of copper, pewter, iron plate, and occasionally silver. The quantity of brass, copper, pewter and iron utensils is usually given merely by weight, and candelabra are not mentioned individually. In August 1548, Paulus Behaim of Nuremberg[137] bought seven brass candlesticks 'to set upon the table'; in December he bought another three 'upon 1 table', with wide bases (obviously larger than

usual); the same year he acquired a set of antlers with four candle-holders for two guilders. Ten years later, he had eight tall brass candle-holders 'with brass saucers' (sconces with dropping-bowls) screwed to the walls of his room.

Distinction was made between drawn wax candles and moulded tallow candles. Only the rich could afford wax candles. In 1507 and during subsequent years, Anton II Tucher obtained more than a hundred white wax candles directly from Venice, for the Dominican Church and for Our Lady's Church at Nuremberg[138]; in 1508, 110 of these cost him seven Rhenish guilders, including transport. In ordinary households, candles made from fat, tallow and other materials of animal origin were used, and these were either produced at home, or obtained from a candle-maker, sometimes with materials derived from home-slaughtered animals. Country people generally slaughtered what they needed to have a year's supply of meat during the cold winter months, and this was the best time for getting a supply of tallow or tallow candles. In the illustrated German-Latin dictionary that has already been mentioned[139] (2nd edition, Nuremberg 1733), the items included for illumination are wax taper, small wax taper, wax candle, light candle, candlestick, a screen, wick, snuffers, lamp, small lamp and small tube for a lamp. The screen attached to a candlestick protected the eye from being dazzled. Snuffers had to be used to trim the wick, otherwise it would begin to smoke. The lamp shown in the book is one we would call a table light, the 'small lamp' a low light bowl (without a foot), whilst the candlestick is an implement with a deep saucer at the base and a ring holder at the top, the kind used with taper-twists. Occasionally a hanging lamp or lantern would be used, bowls of glass or brass with a wick floating in oil, like the sanctuary lamps in churches. In stables, stores and cellars, open lights were not permitted; a lantern was therefore carried or hung up (known as a 'lucerne' on the Upper Rhine).

Fig. 12 Augsburg artist, about 1736: Food and Crockery storage room.
Nuremberg, Germanisches Nationalmuseum.

Fig. 13 Jost Amman: *Der Kupferschmied* (coppersmith). From *Eygentliche Beschreibung aller Stände auf Erden* (Proper Description of All Estates on Earth) by Hans Sachs. Nuremberg, 1568.

Cages and traps

From the fourteenth century, if not before, people kept not only tame animals for use, but also all kinds of tamed creatures and singing birds in cages. Burkhart Münch of Basle had seven large and small cages in 1412[140], and Ludwig Horneck, a young squire in Rufach in Alsace, even had a squirrel cage in 1537[141]. A particularly popular bird was the colourful parrot on its tall perch. From the High Middle Ages it served as the target in shooting competitions, until its place was taken by the eagle during the seventeenth century. Johann Maximilian zum Jungen[142], mayor of Frankfurt, bred canaries in a number of cages; he also had two nightingales. The watchman at Bockenheim spent much time and trouble in 1643 and 1648 training some bullfinches for him. The Baby Houses also have their bird cages, of course.

Rat and mouse-traps of wood or wire supplemented the efforts of the family cat in destroying those nasty rodents. Persistent insects were driven away with long fly-flaps, sometimes even made from peacock's feathers. Paulus Behaim had four made at once from peacock's feathers in 1551[143]. On the painting dated 1476, by the Munich painter Gabriel Mälesskircher, that shows Christ in the house of Simon (now in the Germanischen Nationalmuseum), one of the servants is holding such a fan of peacock's feathers[144]. Comestibles were kept in food-safes protected with wire netting.

Fig. 14 Jost Amman: *Der Kandelgieper* (wax chandler). From the same source as Fig. 13.

The kitchen

12;
61,
104 Housewives took considerable pleasure, in Nuremberg and elsewhere, in having a separate 'state kitchen', not for cooking, but exclusively to display on shelves ranged around the walls one above the other, their stock of shining pewter, brass and copper utensils and also their beautifully decorated faience – a feast for the eyes. 'There you see nothing made of iron or wood, but all must glitter and glisten in pewter and brass, even the broomstick and the dust-basket must be of pewter'[145]. The actual kitchen, being a workroom and housing the hearth, had to be large and spacious. For a long time, cooking was done exclusively on open fires. Hearths where the fire was hidden under an iron plate, with pots and pans placed on holes in the plate, adjusted to size with series of rings, did exist from the middle of the sixteenth century onwards. But hearths of that type were not in general use in Germany at that time. Even so, they were of considerable size. To get the fire to burn well and steadily, the large brick hearth needed a tall chimney that would draw well. Hams and sausages were hung inside the chimney for smoking, and shelves on the outside of the chimney, some of them painted with flowers and foliage, would hold plates, dishes and jugs. The fire was never allowed to go out. As in the living room fireplace, the billets of wood were placed on iron firedogs ('*brandreiten*'), to permit the air to get underneath. In the evening, the embers were drawn together with the fire-hook and a hemispherical lid made of iron bands placed over them. At a later stage, the hearth would have an oven for roasting meat, but this was not to be found everywhere, as meat was roasted on a spit, on the open fire. However, in 1661, Georg Friedrich Behaim[146] had to spend more than three guilders at the locksmiths, 'on account of the small roasting oven at the back'. Pots and pans hung on iron pot-hooks adjustable in height to be nearer or further from flames. Or an iron would be used to suspend the pans, or else they were placed on the tripod amongst the flames. A jack would hold the turning spits. These roasting-jacks really catch the eye in the Baby House kitchens, because they have a mechanism we are no longer familiar with. Bottle-jacks had weights, like a clock, and spring-jacks a spring that could be wound up to keep the spit turning. There were even spits kept in rotation by a dog running in circles, as the *Hauss-Halterin*[147] reports. The roaster-maker

28

27

would come occasionally to undertake cleaning. A range of spits had to be available, to cook anything from large roasts to tiny larks. Sometimes a gridiron would be needed, to grill sausages, for instance. Firepans or chafing dishes were used to provide heat within a more limited compass. These were containers of iron or clay on short legs that were filled with burning charcoal, like the Italian 'scaldini' or the 'stövchen' of Northern Germany.

Hearths and stoves were fired entirely with wood, drying-ovens, warming pans and the like with charcoal, so that there was an enormous demand for these fuels. Town councils were responsible for seeing that sufficient firewood was available for sale, and this would often be quite a problem. Larger cities sometimes had to have their wood brought long distances, by land or by water[148].

Crockery and utensils

The baking utensils left by Severus Korb, cook to Johann Bishop of Strasbourg, in 1608[149] are of some interest: two round wooden moulds bearing the bishop's arms, an elongated wooden mould and a small round earthenware one for 'Fierzücker' (biscuits), a wooden jelly mould that could also be used for that purpose, eight marzipan irons, including one triangular one, two that were square, a heart-shaped and a trefoil-shaped one, three rolling pins and seven wooden wafer rollers, for those popular cakes. In 1521, the Frankfurt patrician Friedrich Stalburg (1469–1524)[150] owned forty 'kuchelstain' (cake-stones), 31 of which he had had engraved, some on both sides, by Hartmann Kistener. These showed a wide variety of designs based on the Old and New Testament, ancient mythology, Medieval literature and popular figures: Adam and Eve, David and Bathsheba, Samson and Delilah, the Adoration, the Three Magi, the Rest on the Flight to Egypt, the Baptism of Christ in the river Jordan, scenes from the Passion,

the Coronation of the Virgin Mary, St Anne, St Christopher, St Mary Magdalen, St Sebastian, St Margaret, 'chaste' Lucretia, Pyramus and Thisbe, Venus with Amor and an old man known as 'No-one', women and fools, a farmer and his wife, 'naked babes', a pair in bed, and all kinds of erotic and other puns and jokes (e.g. a virgin and an old man who is being stung by hornets, and a fool who drives them away for him; a farmer and a virgin who are offering a sackful of fidelity). Eight of the 'stones', four of them with pictures on both sides, are called 'old-Franconian', i.e. they were of an earlier date. Several pieces from this remarkable collection have been preserved.

Crockery and utensils of non-precious metals were usually listed by weight only. The estate of Maria Löffelholz née Sitzinger in 1637[151] included 370 pounds of pewter dishes, 820 pounds of copper and 115 pounds of brass utensils. Even Hans Friederich of Kraftshof, a country place belonging to the Nuremberg patrician family Kress von Kressenstein, left fifteen pounds of pewter and forty pounds of copper utensils in 1586, whereas Joachim Pröbster, farmer at Kraftshof, left only seven pounds of pewter and eleven pounds of copper ware in 1650, shortly after the end of the Thirty Years' War; twelve years later, the smith of Kraftshof, Hans Bröll, left thirteen and a third pounds of copper and fourteen pounds of pewter utensils[152]. It is therefore interesting to note that in 1548 and 1549, Paulus Behaim of Nuremberg, setting up home for himself after the death of his mother, when her estate had been divided between himself and his siblings, listed and bought in new the following[153]: five iron pans, five cooking pots, two water containers of copper, pewter dishes weighing a total of sixteen pounds, a water vessel, two plates, a dish and a flask of pewter plus two plates, two small carving plates, two large dishes, eight small dishes, twelve plates, 36 small plates and a spice box with four compartments, eighty pounds in all of finest 'English' pewter (as

13, 14; 34, 65

Fig. 15 Housewife and Maid. Engraving from *Des hl.Röm. Reichs Stadt Zierdte*, by Johann Alexander Böner. Nuremberg, 1702.

Fig. 16 Laundry. Lithograph from a Nuremberg toy catalogue, second quarter of the nineteenth century.

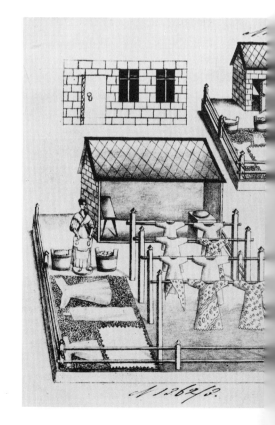

distinct from what was known as Nuremberg or Frankfurt assay, containing no lead), and he also inherited 126 pounds of copper ware and 74 pounds of inferior copper worth fourteen instead of twenty kreutzer the pound.

Paulus Behaim then acquired six cushions and two woven tapestries with green foliage design for a table or bed from Antwerp, and also 24 earthen ('stone') jugs or ewers with pewter lids and three small 'porcelain dishes' (probably European majolica, perhaps from Spain, rather than porcelain from China). Twelve 'broad' wooden plates were for daily use. In 1557, Paulus Behaim bought another fifty large maplewood plates, and had a wooden 'plate basket' made by the turner. In 1551 the trencher-maker made two serving dishes for him, and the painter painted Behaim's arms and those of his wife on these. Willibald Imhoff left twelve such serving dishes in 1580[154], six of them painted, either with ornaments, or with figures and scenery; one of these was red, (which probably means had a red background), and two bore the united arms of him and his wife.

Such plates as could not be accommodated on the shelves – and this meant particularly the simple wooden ones that were used most often – were kept in a painted plate box or in a 'plate case' of wood or wire, one on top of the other, or side by side in vertical compartments. In those days, too, parents often complained of children or servants breaking earthenware dishes and plates. It is probably for this reason that in 1690, Balthasar Kaib of Frankfurt bought four 'lederkoppergen' (leather cups) for his children[155].

With the intention of doing the right and proper thing as a prospective householder, Paulus Behaim acquired a 'painted household-board for the kitchen, whereon one daily writes the expenses' in 1549[156]. This cost him four guilders and 24 kreutzer, a lot of money if one considers that three weeks earlier he had paid the cabinetmaker six guilders for a clothes press; moreover he had had to pay another two guilders to

the locksmith for metal fittings. Only a few of these kitchen and laundry boards are still in existence. The Germanisches Museum has a number of full-size ones painted in several colours, and the Nuremberg Baby Houses also contain a few of them. Anyone unable to read and write could go by the pictures of the things needed for the kitchen – vegetables, meat and bread – or the various items to be washed on wash-day, with a space left next to each for the number, or perhaps also the price, to be entered.

Wash-day

This was always a major undertaking, turning the whole house upside down and upsetting normal daily routine, just like spring-cleaning. In many households the laundry was done only four times a year, sometimes even only twice, in April and September. That was the case in Anton II Tucher's house at Nuremberg during the early sixteenth century[157]. There was no shortage of linen. On one occasion in 1566, Paulus Behaim's wife had 65 large tablecloths washed and 32 small one, 69 towels, 118 napkins and 38 bed-sheets[158]. One or more laundresses would be engaged, for a daily wage and free food. The laundry would have been sorted the day before, the worst of the dirt washed out in cold water, and then the linen was wrung out, and soap and a lye made from oak and beechwood ashes were rubbed into it, to dissolve away more of the dirt during the night. On the great day, hot soapy suds were used, and the laundry rubbed hard, piece by piece and every part of every piece. The wash-tub had a draining hole at the base, to drain off dirty water. Wrung dry once again, the laundry was finally transferred to a tub filled with hot water and a special soap made by boiling together animal residues and soapstone. After rubbing it all again, it was boiled in a large boiler and finally thoroughly rinsed, some of it starched, and hung out to dry. When dry, large and small

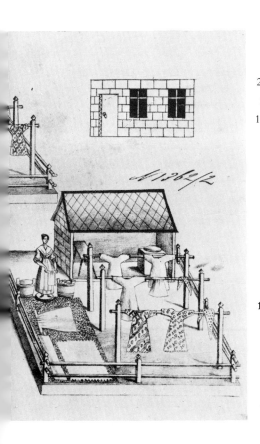

pieces were folded on the straight, or pulled straight on a table and folded and rolled up. Coloureds would not be put to soak overnight, nor were they left in water for any length of time, treated with lye, or boiled. Soap was coming to be more and more widely used, but many people still washed exclusively with lye made from ashes. Bucking was a method that saved a great deal of soap, and one also did not have to rub the laundry; on the other hand it required more firewood, The method consisted in placing a tall washtub with provision for drainage at the bottom on top of another one. A large sheet was placed on the bottom, and the dirty linen put on top of this and soaked in plain water overnight. After draining off the water in the morning, a coarse 'ash-cloth' was spread over the washing. Wood-ash was sprinkled onto this and boiling water poured over. The lye thus produced passed through the ash-cloth and acted on the wash. After a time, the hot lye was run off and poured over the top again. The procedure was repeated several times, and if necessary the linen was after that washed with soap as well[159]. Wooden clothes-pegs were used to peg out the wash, and presses and mangles to calender it, whilst smoothing irons would be used for the finer body linen. In 1580[160], Willibald Imhoff's wash-house contained the following: 2 casks, 1 trestle and cask, 3 vats and 2 small vats, 2 washtubs, 1 small tub, 1 wooden bucket, 1 large lye bucket, laundry baskets and laundry tables, as well as two presses for the linen.

Bath-house and privy

Another important institution to be found in upper middle-class households was the bathroom. In the 1611 Baby House, the painting on the right-hand door in the basement, showing a maid with a child already undressed for the bath, indicates that the bathroom could not be far away. The large copper used to heat the water was usually firmly cemented into the

brick-stove. An inventory from Wildungen dated 1612[161] refers to a bath boiler of six buckets capacity on the stove. Another of twice that size had an iron base and stood on the floor. Large dippers were used to fill the bath-tub. The poem on household goods previously mentioned (Strasbourg 1514)[162] refers to a straw tent that was placed over the bath-tub whilst herbs placed in the hot water encouraged perspiration to cleanse the skin. Afterwards one would be able to rest on the benches that ran round the walls of the bathroom. The walls were supposed to have wood-panelling, so that one would not catch a chill by leaning against cold stonewalls when heated from the bath[163].

The 'privy chamber' or 'secret', the dark private corner, often situated under the stairs, must also be mentioned. Examples are to be found in some of the earlier Baby Houses. At long intervals, probably no more frequently than once a year, it was 'swept'. In Nuremberg, the 'night-masters' who came to perform this office at dark of night were known as 'pappenheimer'. Beneath the beds stood pewter night vessels, for which there were a number of names, – there was one in the 1558 Munich Baby House – and close-stools, also called 'occasion', 'room', 'prophey' or 'utterance' stools, were also used.

The servants

'No house-mother can remain without menials, and it is not proper for ladies of the higher classes to do all the maids' work, not to mention that this work is so great and varied that even one and another servant cannot accomplish it; in the lower classes housekeeping is often as complex as in higher ones, wherefore they must look about to have one or more maids'. Thus the Hauss-Halterin in 1703[164]. More well-to-do families usually had at least three maids, a housemaid to do the cleaning and see to the linen, a cook, possibly with a kitchen-maid to assist, and a nursery maid.

Fig. 17 Augsburg artist, about 1736: Maids' Room.
Nuremberg, Germanisches Nationalmuseum.

Fig. 18 Title page from *Die so kluge als künstliche ... Hauss-Halterin*. Nuremberg, 1703.

Housewives used to have many problems with their servants, called 'ehehalten' in Nuremberg, or with the lack of servants. Three police regulations concerning servants were issued in 1530, 1548 and 1577. To stop them from running away without leave, a reference was made a condition for getting a new position. The Imperial estates were urged to issue regulations for servants, and one such set of regulations appeared in print in Nuremberg in 1628. The question of domestic agencies had been dealt with by the town council a hundred years earlier, with a number of older women acting in that capacity. Wage scales were firmly established. According to the tariff issued in Frankfurt in 1623 and 1654, a female cook received nine or ten guilders a year, a housemaid or chambermaid six or seven, a children's nursemaid four or five[165]. Even with bed and board provided, and here and there also items of clothing given, such wages seem extraordinarily low to us. For comparison, some prices that can be assessed in present-day terms are given. In 1622, Lukas Friedrich Behaim[116] paid two guilders for two canaries; his son Georg Friedrich paid seven guilders for 36 yards of 'Linz cloth' for shifts (23.80 metres of linen) in 1658[167], and fifteen guilders and forty kreutzers for four and a half yards (approx. three metres) of black (wool) cloth in 1662. A 'maid's cloak' cost him three guilders and thirty kreutzers in 1666, and a coif bought for the maid in December of that year, 52 kreutzers. In 1663, Christoph Kress[168] bought three pieces of 'wurschat' (worsted) 'to clothe the maids' for sixteen guilders and thirty kreutzers, fustian 'to clothe the gardener' for four guilders and fifteen kreutzers, and also paid four guilders and fifty kreutzers to 'clothe' the fisherman at Kraftshof, plus seven guilders and ten kreutzers 'for caps for the maids'.

Servants did however receive frequent tips and money presents; some of these, such as the New Year and (in Frankfurt) the fair gift, were their due and mentioned as such in their contracts. In 1661 Georg Friedrich Behaim gave his maid a 'kindleinsbescher' (Christ-child gift) of four guilders. Her quarterly wage was two guilders and thirty kreutzers, making a total of ten guilders per annum. With tips for running errands she was probably able to increase this annual sum by half as much again. During the seventeenth century, a maid had few desires (or perhaps was able to have only a few desires?) as regards possessions and simple pleasures. Many left their wages in the hands of their masters. to accrue interest year after year, a clear indication that the money was not needed for current expenditure.

In many places there was a constant coming and going of servants. Mistresses used to complain that they were slow and indolent, rebellious and impertinent, dirty or negligent. Hans Sachs' tales of thieving and lazy servants, Peter Gasser's *Gesindeteufel* (servant devil) of 1566, Abraham a Santa Clara's sermons (1644 – 1709), some broadsheets, and details given in old letters and housekeeping journals tell many a tale. Of course there were also faithful, honest and reliable 'ehehalten' (menials). Their virtues were however taken for granted, and it is only the unsatisfactory servant one hears about. All in all, servants probably were no worse than they were expected to be.

The number of persons due to receive a gift of money from a well-to-do householder each time the New Year came round was considerable. In 1662, Georg Friedrich Behaim[169] gave three guilders to the preacher at Our Lady's Church, more than a guilder each to the father confessor (in the Protestant church, confession was not abolished until the eighteenth century, with the Age of Enlightenment), to Mr W.I. Müller, and to the two maids of Tobias Tucher, the father of his first wife. Other recipients of carefully graded smaller sums were the steeple-watchmen at St Sebaldus' Church, and the watchmen at three of the city gates, the manservant at the town hall, the messenger to the chancery, the waiters at the council chamber and chancery, the sacristans of four local churches, the barber's men, the chimney sweeps, the shopkeeper's boy, the brewer's man, and the ostlers at the mews.

Everyday life at home

What was everyday life like in a middle-class household three or four hundred years ago? People of all classes would rise very early, to make the most of the daylight, as candles and small oil lamps provided a light that by our standards was very poor indeed. One therefore rose at four or five in the morning, during the darker winter months sometimes not until six o'clock. After getting dressed, both Catholics and Protestants would hold morning prayers. Ernest the Pious, Duke of Saxony-Gotha (1601–75)[170] insisted that his children rise at six a.m. all the year round, only the youngest being allowed an extra hour in bed. After prayers, they had to wash and clean their teeth. Toothpowder, by the way, was available as early as the sixteenth century. Each of the four German students we have already mentioned at Padua in around 1585 (three young Fuggers and Wolf, Count of Montfort[171]) possessed a small silver box to contain it, and also a tooth-scraper. After washing, dressing and prayers, the morning soup would be eaten, sometimes with bread, eggs and meat or fish served as well. Artisans would start work at six a.m. at the latest. The midday meal would therefore be taken early, between 11 and 12 o'clock; it was certainly over by 12 o'clock. The hot evening meal was put on the table between five and six p.m. According to Hippolytus Guarinonius (1571–1654), a Tyrolean physician[172], it was advisable to retire at eight o'clock, or nine o'clock at the latest, to get a good night's sleep.

All the activities and events that made up the life of the housewife, or house-mother as she was often called at that time, everything that filled the narrow frame of her days, would take place between six in the morning and eight o'clock at night. She lived in the house and entirely for the house, this was her domain, complete in itself, with the daily tasks that filled her life. She cared for her own family and those belonging to it as maids and manservants, shared the personal joys and sorrows of friends and family, visiting those who were in child-bed, attending christenings, weddings and funerals, giving birth to her usually numerous children, rearing them, being responsible for order and cleanliness in house and kitchen, yard and garden, taking care of and adding to the household goods, and running her house with due care and regard.

The house-mother was to 'instruct her daughters well in the work of house and kitchen, that they shall know how to prepare both everyday meals and special delicacies, to treat all kinds of baked goods and confectionery, arrange a banquet, and fittingly array table and dresser for this, and indeed know how to manage and give orders concerning everything that may occur in a household . . . yet is that which serves the general housekeeping most necessary above all, it being ill indeed if a woman has to let the maid proceed as she will, or, there being need to correct or reprove her, is unable to do such thing better herself or indicate where the fault does lie.'[173] Thus the *Hauss-Halterin* in 1703. The future housewife first of all needed to be instructed in the art of housekeeping herself. The Baby Houses were intended to demonstrate everything connected with the house as such, every single item of furniture and equipment, with the laundry, utensils, their proper management and use. This included the acquisition of new pieces, chosen carefully and in good time, keeping things clean and in good order, with regular inspection, the proper preparation, storage and utilization of stocks and provisions for house and kitchen, and the management of fires and lights. Daughters had to learn to handle linen and silk, cotton and wool correctly, they had to gain experience in the care of children, of the sick

Fig. 19 Women at work in the kitchen. Engraving from *Georgica Curiosa*, by Johann von Hohberg. Nuremberg, 1701.

and of those in child-bed. Nor must they neglect their personal hygiene. Added to this was looking after the garden, its flowers, plants and fruit trees, which included knowledge of local weather conditions. Finally the animals in and around the house also required due care and attention.

Economic conditions were totally different from today. Here and there they may have remained much the same until the first half of the present century, but it is extraordinarily difficult to gain a concrete idea of conditions in those days. There certainly was no question of living from hand to mouth, of shopping just for today and tomorrow. Provisions were normally bought in large quantities and stored in the cellar and store rooms. Fruits and vegetables came from the market, unless of course they were home-grown, or were imported from the south occasionally to add a touch of luxury to the table. Poultry was slaughtered at home, and sometimes also pigs, cattle and sheep, or meat was bought at the butcher's, usually in large pieces. Sausages would then be made at home, and foods were dried, pickled, candied, made into preserves, and put up in vinegar, salt and marinades. If butter was not made at home, it would as a rule be bought only at considerable intervals, but then in large quantities, and usually salt and salt water were all that were available to help one keep it, with no actual means of refrigeration. The cellars would normally be cool, however, and some people probably had ice cut in winter and kept it in covered pits and ice-cellars to provide cold storage during the warmer months of the year.

Where bread was not baked at home, the baker provided a daily supply of this staple. There was also plenty to do with the brewing of beer and mead, making up fruit, herb and spiced wines, preparing cordials, vinegar and essences. Candle-making has already been mentioned, and in many households soap was made as well, or at least bought soap improved by adding all kinds of tinctures and scents; indeed

housewives even knew how to make scented gloves, using ambergris, civet, musk, and rose or orange flower water[174].

Craftsmen would be called in for various repairs and overhauls. The roaster-master not only had to clean the roaster, but also replace the springs now and then. The cooper would put new hoops on tubs and vats. The slater or tiler came to 'overclimb' the roof and check it for holes. The gutters, eaves and well (there was of course no water from a tap) were cleaned, chimneys, stoves and hearths swept. In line with the general economic pattern of the time, much more was bought directly from the craftsman than from a shop. The cabinet-maker made furniture to order, the locksmith the keys and fittings to go with it, the purse-maker provided leather covers for chairs and seats, other items were obtained from the spur-maker, the smith and the goldsmith, the mould-maker who carved the wooden moulds for marzipan and small cakes, the turner, saddler and grinder. The shoemaker must not be forgotten, for he put on soles and also made new shoes. Artisans would also be called on for bleaching and dyeing, weaving and tapestry-making, unless these crafts were carried out at home. The accounts of craftsmen who did regular work were frequently paid only at the end of the year.

There were innumerable household recipes for the cleaning and care of household equipment and utensils, and for remedies in sickness, as well as for body-care and beauty products. These were mixed and prepared at home, from herbs, seeds and extracts, whereas today we depend almost entirely on manufactured products.

198

The garden

Herbs, vegetables and flowers were as far as possible grown in one's own garden, developed from the herb garden of the Middle Ages. Joy and pride in one's garden flourished everywhere during the sixteenth and seventeenth centuries. Where possible,

Fig. 20   The Peller Garden at Nuremberg. Engraving, 1655.

a small garden would be cultivated immediately behind the house, whilst the large kitchen, fruit and vegetable plot was outside the city walls, beyond the gate. The garden by the house was usually entirely for pleasure. Bien's watercolours of the house of the Teutonic Knights at Nuremberg (1625)[175] show very formal gardens with geometrically designed beds, trimmed espaliers and shrubberies, with only here and there a full-crowned tree bringing life into the geometric structure. During the summer, flowers from the south would also be grown, and orange trees in large tubs, painted red in many cases, were placed on either side of paths that were always kept incredibly tidy. There was no lack of flowers – in the Middle Ages, roses, lilies, lily-of-the-valley, columbines and others were widely grown – but the sheer joy in such blooms, the pleasure of having them around and adorning both oneself and one's home with them, to grow them on terraces and balconies and train them up trellises – all this did not come in until the Renaissance. Then one finds 'greenery jars', the flowerboxes of that time, in inventories. In 1559, Heinrich Herwarth of Augsburg is said to have brought the first tulips from Constantinople to Germany[176]. In 1576, the first German crown imperial flowers were grown in the imperial gardens at Vienna. Many people had great ambitions, to produce evermore beautiful and new varieties, obtaining seeds and cuttings from far distant places. Thus the large yard of the 1611 Nuremberg Baby House naturally has a formally laid-out ornamental garden, and in the case of the House painted with white tendrils on a red background, the eye is drawn from the yard to the long vista of a formal garden, albeit only painted. The great Dutch Baby Houses of the late seventeenth and early eighteenth century also have their gardens or a view of the garden.

As to vegetables, it was during the sixteenth and seventeenth centuries that some of those we now consider delicacies were introduced, not by professional gardeners,

but by ordinary citizens who took pleasure in gardening. The first reference to asparagus in Nuremberg is dated 1557, when Paulus Behaim grew it in his garden. Since then, the northern part of the area around Nuremberg, the 'garlic' country, has become well known for its asparagus. The first artichokes appeared in Nuremberg in 1569, and in 1576 Willibald Imhoff bought cauliflower seed. During the seventeenth and eighteenth centuries, some of the gardens in Nuremberg were famous well beyond the confines of the city, examples being the Peller gardens, and the highly scientific 'Horticultura' of Johann Christoph Volkamer[177].

Needlework

'A sensible mother desiring her daughters to prosper shall spare no effort, trouble and expenditure'[178], to instruct them or have them instructed in all the female arts and crafts, in sewing, knitting, embroidery, in bobbin-lace-making, silk-weaving with the batten, ribbon-weaving, in passementerie, in the skilful turning of cords, in the making of tassels and fringes. There is documentary evidence[179] that paper patterns were used for cutting out from the sixteenth century, with all the sewing done neatly by hand. Apart from work bespoken from professional tailors and dressmakers, sewing women, men and women embroiderers, there was still a great deal done at home – incredible amounts of needlework by present-day standards.

In November 1624, Lukas Friedrich Behaim bought a sampler for his eldest daughter Sabina, then nine years old; this cost twelve kreutzers, and he spent two guilders and twelve kreutzers on embroidery silks for her. In 1629, the same daughter was given 'Leonic gold' (gold thread) and 'bones' (bobbins), in 1632, materials for gold embroidery[180]. From the second half of the sixteenth century onwards, girls learned to embroider on samplers, usually of unbleached linen, using patterns from printed pattern books, their own designs

Fig. 21 Women doing embroidery and spinning. Engraving from *Georgica Curiosa*, by Johann von Hohberg. Nuremberg, 1701.

Fig. 22 Noble lady before a stand of secondhand goods. Engraving from *Des hl. Röm. Reichs Stadt Zierdte*, by Johann Alexander Böner. Nuremberg, 1702.

and those of others: embroidery in white and coloured threads, with all kinds of stitches – stem-stitch, tent-stitch, chain-stitch, cross-stitch and its variations, satin-stitch and tapestry stitch, knot stitch, buttonhole stitch, cut and drawn-thread work. The letters of the alphabet and the numbers from 1 to 10 were popularly embroidered on these samplers, often in a variety of designs; the young embroideress would also add her name, or perhaps just her initials, and the year, also decorative borders, numerous arrangements of flowers and fruits, lions and stags, small bright birds and a peacock in full display, armorial beasts such as the double eagle, castles with turrets and towers, Adam and Eve under the tree in Paradise, the Crucifixion, the Instruments of the Passion, the Pascal Lamb, and many other things[181]. During 1647–8, the nineteen-year-old daughter of Johann Maximilian zum Jungen, mayor of Frankfurt, received instruction in cushion embroidery. For a fee of six guilders, the painter Lorenz Müller had designed patterns for six cushions. The coloured silks used in the embroidery cost the girl's father almost forty guilders. In addition, he paid 'Frau Anna Maria Faber, widow, for 32 weeks (not counting the midday meal and sometimes also of an evening), that she has taught my daughter Anna Christina to sew with silks upon satin and canvas, and also herself done sewing on the cushions with armorial bearings, at two guilders each, altogether 64 guilders'. Somewhat more than five guilders had to be spent on further wages and for New Year's gifts.

Cushions, covers and chair seats were embroidered, also curtains and carpets, books and small boxes, cases and comb-cases, bedlinen, table-linen and towels, dresses, aprons, shifts, kerchiefs and handkerchiefs, gloves, and indeed shoes and stockings; these and many other garments and household items were embellished with designs in one or several colours, rich or delicate. But there were also all kinds of other skills and handicrafts for women. Just a few shall be mentioned from the 26

chapters giving full details in the *Hauss-Halterin*: artificial flowers and fruits in the 'welsh' style, made from linen; silk flowers wound with the aid of gum tragacanth; wax flowers and fruits; cases that were gilded and decorated with flowers, and also fruits, made from a kind of papier-mâché; work in coloured straw; 'castor work' (flowers, fruit and foliage of wool or silk dust on linen, similar to flock-paper hangings) to make pictures but also to decorate larger areas such as folding screens[183].

A housewife was also supposed to know and distinguish the different types of fabric in use at that time, such as 'Catoun' (chintz) or 'Nesseltuch' (nettle cloth). The latter, in a tabby weave, was 'quite thin and loose-woven … serving both male and female persons at times for all kinds of adornment and decking out'. 'Catoun' was coarser – there was also 'Half Catoun' – ('of cotton and linen thread intermingled'). 'Use is made of this not only for various types of dresses, but also for espaliers, carpets, curtains and other such'. Fabrics of half cotton and entirely of cotton were 'improved' by printing in black or one or several colours. Another material of half cotton and half linen was 'Bomasin' (bombasine), the 'plain or striped or block-printed fustian', the first being used mostly for bed-ticking, the other two 'for all kinds of clothes'.

Dyed linen was called 'Schetter', and there were several kinds of this. Starched black 'Schetter' (buckram) was 'commonly used only beneath button-holes, to give them hold, that they may not fray and tear so soon'. The 'softer black one', and others in green, yellow, red, brown and other broken colours served 'chiefly as underlining for clothes, and people of the lower classes as well as servants also wear upper clothing of it'. Finally blue 'Schetter', both light and dark blue, was much calendered and ironed, to give it a good sheen, and 'mostly worn and used for aprons by the women of the artisan class'[184].

63

The day's work done

The bustling day, with its toil and trouble, was complemented by leisure time, with games and sociability. In the present context, mention cannot be made of the many popular entertainments such as the annual fair, the May festival, animal shows, the performances of tightrope walkers and strolling players, lotteries and raffling shops, but merely of leisure hours spent among family and friends. Growing sons were given instruction in drawing and fencing and learned to play an instrument. Music-making was general, and the 1514 Strasbourg poem on household goods lists several instruments. On the wall paintings in the lower hall of the oldest of the Nuremberg Baby Houses, people are dining, wining and making music. The 1639 Baby House has a small spinet. Lukas Friedrich Behaim regularly went to his 'music circle'. According to outgoings for repairs written up in his housekeeping journal, he owned a small house-organ ('positive'), a viola and a lute[185]. In 1619, he had a spinet made by Paul Wissmayer of which only the lid is still in existence. At the centre, four string-players are accompanied by the basso continuo on the spinet, and around these are illustrations of the four seasons in the area around Nuremberg[186]. Lutes are commonly mentioned in the inventories, usually with their cases, and also flutes, dulcimers, fiddles, etc. Music was simply part of life, everyone played instruments and sang in choirs of many voices.

One would also be a member of a sociable 'circle' where one enjoyed conversation and merry games. Adults in particular played many games, with cards, and the 'tower' game already mentioned, requiring cards and a special board, later also 'poke' and of course chess, draughts and backgammon, games needing special figures or stones; from the turn of the sixteenth to the seventeenth century onwards also the game of the goose[187]. This is the grandfather of all dice games, with hindering and helping

positions on a spiral proceeding from square 1 to 63 in a large field. In 1617, the Augsburg patrician and diplomat Philipp Hainhofer played the game of the goose several times when staying with the Duke and Duchess in Pomerania. His written records indicate the social status of the game at that time. In 1626, Lukas Friedrich Behaim acquired a game of the goose[188]. Maria Löffelholz née Sitzinger appears to have owned a particularly handsome board for this game, for it is listed among the paintings forming part of her estate in 1637[189] and valued at four guilders.

Dolls and puppets for the children

The children had their 'Dockenwerk' (doll or puppet things) which they received for Christmas, New Year or Twelfth Day, sometimes also at Easter: balls, tops, marbles, hoops, kites, wind-wheels, and also dolls, horses and carts, hobby-horses, all kinds of animals, hunts, miniature models of clothing, handkerchiefs, and also ginger bread, sweet chestnuts, a savings box, a the list of Christmas gifts that Sabina Löffelholz, née Harsdorffer, chose for her children in 1619, the first year of her widowhood[190]. She had brought ten children into the world, nine of whom were still living. The four bigger ones, aged twelve to eighteen, received mostly items of clothing, handkerchiefs, and also gingerbread, sweet chestnuts, a savings box, a wax-taper, paper, ink, a whistle or a knife; eleven-year-old John was also given a sailing boat, seven-year-old Barbara a doll's cradle and all that went with it and a '*henssla buben*' (boy doll), a spinning wheel, a cake-mixing bowl, pots, jugs, dishes, a copper flask etc., no doubt to play dolls with; five-year-old Maria Salome received a doll and cart, three-year-old Anna Maria a boy doll, a basket to be carried on the arm, a slate, a violin, and finally one-year-old Catharina, among other gifts, a doll and a rattle. The garments Frau Löffelholz gave to her children were just as stiff and severe in cut and material as those worn by

Fig. 23 Housewife, maid and children outside the front door. Woodcut from *Curioser Spiegel*, by Elias Porcelius. Nuremberg, about 1689.

adults at that time. Children always went about dressed as miniature adults. Day after day they had before their eyes what they were supposed to achieve. The Baby Houses were also intended to serve that end, at least those in Southern Germany. Mirrors of their time, they present the domestic life of the period and are better able today to give us a good idea of that life than anything else.

Baby Houses at Nuremberg, Strasbourg, Basle, Ulm and Augsburg

So far, we have considered in detail only the two Nuremberg Baby Houses from the first half of the seventeenth century. The 44– House owned by the Bäumler family (225
53 × 177.5 × 68cm) is the only one with its façade, complete with its oriel at the centre of the first floor, still intact. It had been completely painted over in a light beige in 1829. The original ox-blood colour with cartouches and borders in white and grey,
53 combined with flowers and branches painted in orange on the outside and large white tendrils on the inside walls, seemed too garish to the people of the Biedermeier period. With the original paint from the
47 second half of the seventeenth century restored, this House has regained much of its former character. On both sides some light can enter through the two bottle-glass windows on each floor. The furnishings have undergone considerable changes in several of the rooms. Only the parlour on the first
49 floor and a small room at the centre of the second floor, next to the magnificent state kitchen, are panelled; the two landings, the
53 large room on the second floor, and the yard are painted. With its walls now showing their original red colour, the yard forms a whole complete in itself, opening onto the painted vista of a garden.

The twin gables of the Baby House
54– formerly owned by the Kress von Kressen-
59 steins, a patrician family, probably did not form part of the House originally. Nuremberg dwelling houses did not have such double gables facing the street. Could it be

that the two gables now facing the front 55 were originally facing the sides, so that the roof rose at an angle above the façade, as in the case of the 1639 and the Bäumler Houses? But the dimensions of the gable would then no longer agree with those of the house, and the gables must have come from a House about 70cm in depth, whereas this House is 139cm long and only 53.5cm deep. A particularly attractive feature are the tall balustrades of turned 56/ wood. Those of the 1611 Baby House have 57 unfortunately been lost, whilst in the 1639 House they have been largely replaced with 26, flat, cut-out balusters painted to indicate a 28 third dimension. The handsome balusters of the Kress House not only delimit each room to the front, but also form balustrades on the landings and balconies around the yard, at the centre of the ground floor. The furnishings and arrangement of the House are of the usual type seen in the Nuremberg Baby Houses of the seventeenth to eighteenth century. Various items have been added during the eighteenth century, particularly the dolls with wax 54 heads.

The Houses still to be found at Nuremberg today are by and large the same in external design as Anna Köferlin's 1631 **1** House. Another smaller one of the type is in the Victoria and Albert Museum's annexe at Bethnal Green[191]. This house, with its façade, dates back to 1673; its dimensions are 106.5 × 92.2 × 45.7cm, and it has four rooms, in two stories, the 60/ kitchen and state kitchen below, and two 61 rooms, each with a bed, above. A fifth house at the Germanisches National-museum is not actually a house, but a 32– cabinet with a drawer beneath, a large 36 kitchen below, and a room with particu- 42/ larly attractive furnishings above. The tall 43 green stove has alternately tiles with flower-vases beneath round arches and 42 balusters terminating in a bust of a female 32, figure. Blue and white fan-shaped dishes of 35 Nuremberg faience alternate with turned and painted ornaments along the top of the wainscoting. The bedding piled high on

the bed is covered with white, blue-and-
32 white chequered, diamond-patterned and
blue-printed bedlinen. There are two cup-
43 boards with three-storey top structures,
cut-out decorations, moulded and flaming-
fillets. All kinds of pewter utensils bearing
34 the Nuremberg hallmark have been
arranged on these and also in the kitchen.

The two 'Baby Houses' at Strasbourg
and Basle are actually built into proper
70– cupboards. The former bears the date 1681
76 at the top of the door to the room at the left
of the lower floor, 1678 on a cupboard,
and 1680 on the door upstairs[192]. The
72 arrangement of the rooms cannot be said to
correspond to that of an actual house.
74 Downstairs, the wide yard with stable and
draw-well is flanked by a small sitting-room
containing two cupboards typical for the
Upper Rhine region, one of them designed
as a high dresser ('trisur', as it was called in
Alsace). The kitchen and the second parlour above are of equal size. Both have
73– bottle-glass windows at the back – some-
75 thing one does not see in Nuremberg

Houses, but no light can actually enter
through those windows.

In the Basle cabinet[193], the cellar with its 77–
various sections is below, with the kitchen 84
and finally the sitting-room above it. The 78–
latter has a board floor and a painted ceil- 80
ing. Above the wainscot, colourful flowers
and foliage decorate the walls in a broad
band. The dresser, painted the same as the
wainscot, and the other heavy furniture
come from the seventeenth century; on the
other hand, in the kitchen, a large hearth of 83/
green glazed pottery dated 1768 has recent- 84
ly been added.

From the Figdor Collection comes an
'Ulm' Baby House in Vienna[194]. But this
merely consists of some beautiful old furniture and domestic items that were restored
in the nineteenth century, with a house
built around them. In the House at the
museum in Ulm[195], too, only a few pieces 197–
go back to the seventeenth century. The 205
Augsburg House at the Bayerisches
Nationalmuseum in Munich was built during the late seventeenth century[196].

The Dutch Houses

The Baby Houses and cabinets from seventeenth century Southern Germany represent middle-class homes of that period on a miniature scale, and nothing, seemingly, has been forgotten. Looking at them with some perception, the whole domestic life of those times unfolds before one's inner eye. The elegant Dutch Houses from the late seventeenth and the first half of the eighteenth century may be said to go one step further. The Houses preserved at Utrecht, Amsterdam, The Hague and Haarlem either are cabinets or are built into cabinets. They cannot be considered mere object lessons, but are indeed items for ostentatious display. It appears that the Nuremberg Cabinet at Pottendorf in Lower Austria, known to us only from an inventory[197], was similarly a cabinet piece; but all the South-German Baby Houses still in existence also served to a certain extent as object lessons. They are solidly middle-class, as distinct from the upper middle-class ostentation and intricacy of the Dutch Houses. The difference may in the final instance be sociological in origin.

Petronella de la Court's House

Thanks to research carried out in Holland during the fifties, the history of the various Houses in existence there has been well established, greatly emphasizing the individual character of each House. One of the oldest is a House in the Centraal Museum at Utrecht, dated between 1674 and 1690[198]. With its stand of four short twisted walnut columns and olive-wood cabinet, it has a total height of 206.5cm, is 182cm long, and 74.5cm deep. It was made for Petronella de la Court in Amsterdam. A German travelling in Holland, Zacharias Konrad von Uffenbach, saw it on 18 March 1711[199]. He speaks of a visit to Mrs de la Court, wife of a dyer, but in this he must have been mistaken. He no doubt visited the house of Petronella Oortman and her husband, the merchant Abraham du Pré; it was the mother Petronella who was a de la Court by birth, and she had the House built.

Uffenbach's account gives a most interesting description of the environment in which he found the Baby House, in the home of a passionate and knowledgeable collector. 'First she showed us some good depictions (pictures), and then three small rooms full of porcelain, of which she made much. She assured us that Prince Eugenius had spent half a day looking at this porcelain... She also showed us a great number of perforated rinsing bowls, in various sizes, of which she had a dozen white. She showed us also what is known as paternoster ware; also with armorial bearings, further jugs with snouts, all of which, as she assured us, cost a terrible sum of money. We particularly had to admire twelve small flower jars for which she had paid twelve thousand guilders. All her porcelain was also blue and white... Up above she had a glass cupboard in which there were all kinds of small doll's things, as the Dutch call it, such as according to her is best made in Haarlem. After which she showed us her cabinet, where we first of all saw a quite uncommon store of generated stones. Most of these were modern, but so precious and in such quantity ... She also had many vessels of Oriental agate and porphyry... Further she showed us a box in which there were many mother-of-pearl shells, all cut by Bellekins, handsomer than any we had ever seen ... Furthermore she had two small pictures, finger-long, cut in coral ... Furthermore she showed us three pieces of ivory, affixed to black velvet. They were bas reliefs, uncommonly well cut by Francis (van Bossuit; 1635–92). She also had the twelve first emperors with their consorts, engraved very neatly in mother-of-pearl by Bellekins and inset with black... She also showed us a box with all kinds and varieties of precious stones ... She showed us also a death's-head of amber, the size of a Welsh nut, transparent and marvellously made. Then she showed us her medals ... She herself asserted, and one may well believe it, that her curiosities cost her more than a hundred thousand guilders.' In this to our

86–95

minds quite amazing collection, the doll's cabinet is more or less mentioned only in passing. Then as now, it had glass doors. The letters AO on the elaborately carved bench in the first-floor vestibule refer to Adam Oortman, father of Petronella du Pré and husband of Petronella de la Court, who was the owner of the Swan Brewery at Amsterdam. The mother also had an unusual collection of paintings and drawings, prints and rarities. At the auction held in Amsterdam in October 1707, after her death, the paintings of Dutch masters, the porcelain and other cabinet pieces, brought in 35,155 guilders. The drawings and prints probably went to a new owner en bloc. Only the Baby House and a Netherlands atlas of nine volumes, which, as her will of 7 January 1697 shows, were obviously particularly dear to the lady, remained in the possession of her children. The Baby House therefore became part of her daughter's collection, a daughter who had inherited the collector's instinct from her mother. After the death of Petronella Oortman and Abraham du Pré, that collection was also to be sold. The Baby House was put on public offer both in 1730 and in 1736, but it appears there were no takers, and it was not until 1744 that it was finally acquired by Pieter von der Beek, who bought it for his wife, Maria Sophia Heykoop. Her daughter Margaretha, married to Dirk Slob, had a catalogue of the House printed as a 'guide' for visitors, as was then customary in Holland. In 1866, her grand-daughter, then resident in Utrecht, presented the House to that city.

87 The eleven rooms of the Utrecht House occupy three floors, with the most elegant rooms in the middle storey. Below, the
88 spacious kitchen with its Dutch open
89 hearth is followed by the lying-in room and a garden. A water chamber and the 'secreet' are built in at the back of the kitchen. The kitchen has a subtle air of exquisiteness, and this not only because of the fine glasses displayed on shelves hung on the left wall, or the porcelain collected on the turned shelf-unit on the opposite side of the room. The lying-in room has a linen cupboard on a stand of six tall twisted legs; the doors are decorated with figures of Faith and Hope carved in relief in ivory. 92 The seats and backs of the chairs of turned ivory are covered in bright silk. The table-cloth, and the shoulder-cape and decorative apron worn by the lying-in woman are richly trimmed with bobbin-lace. A painted Fortuna, ascribed to Gérard de Lairesse (1641–1711) adorns the high chimney breast. Three of the pictures on the walls, those of Cardinal Mazarin, Louis XIV and his queen Maria Theresia, have probably been added during the eighteenth century. The garden has a delicate 87 ornamental pavilion among flowers and plants. This is as beautifully carved of ivory as the allegorical figures representing the four seasons placed around it on tall open-work pedestals. Dolls in the costumes of the late seventeenth century add life to all the rooms of the House. In the vestibule on the first floor, a gentleman and a children's nurse holding a child on a long leading rein almost completely hide the tall English clock by Théodore Arnaud with its case covered in tortoiseshell. The four winds are painted on the ceiling, and the floor has a pattern of black and white marble slabs. The four ivory reliefs with themes from antique mythology were probably also added during the eighteenth century. Two busts framed in black on the wall at the back represent Minerva and Mercury, patrons of science and commerce. Above the vestibule is the counting-room of the master of the house where 94 he sits in his dressing-gown at his writing table, surrounded by folios and papers. The walls and ceiling of the reception room 90 on the left side of the first floor are covered by large paintings on canvas by Frederick de Moucheron (1633–86). A distinguished company dressed in the latest Paris fashions is assembled, making music or being entertained with music. Even more such valuable items are to be seen in the art cabinet on the right side of the first floor. The room has a parquet floor, made from a

Fig. 24 House-painters at work. Woodcut from *Curioser Spiegel*, by Elias Porcelius. Nuremberg, about 1689.

variety of woods. Coloured copper etchings have been used to decorate the ceiling, with the four elements shown on either side, around an angel at the centre surrounded by the four winds. The paintings hung on the walls are by Gerard Hoet (1648–1733) bearing the date 1674, Jan van Hughtenburgh (1647–1733), and Willem van Mieris (1662–1747) dated 1682. The top of a table of amber with a carved stand abounding with acanthus leaf decorations, has a delicate inlaid ivory relief. A cabinet with glass doors contains some beautiful porcelain from East Asia, and another with marquetry work of various woods and ivory holds a collection of rarities made of silver and ivory. A miniature celestial globe and a statue of Mercury are also made of ivory. The top floor has a storage room on the left and a linen room on the right, where the ironing· is being done and which also contains a linen press. Between those two rooms are the nursery and the bedroom. In the nursery, the floor is covered with straw-matting and the walls in red silk. A coloured engraving by Hendrick Goltzius on the ceiling shows the personification of autumn. The reliefs on the silver stove represent Abraham as host to the three Strangers, and on the other side, three people around a fire. In the bedroom, floor and walls are covered in silk, and the ceiling has a coloured engraving with the apotheosis of the emperor Leopold I. The battle scene on the chimney breast is ascribed to J. van Hughtenburgh, around 1690. There are also pictures by W. van Mieris, Daniel Vertangen (1598–1681 –84) and Pieter van Slingeland (1640–91). The tester-bed with its curtains, the table-cloth, the chair seats and backs of precious silks are trimmed with fringes and tassels, or with white bobbin-lace.

Petronella Oortman's House

The Baby House of Petronella Oortman, wife of Jacob Brandt, now at the Rijksmuseum in Amsterdam[200], is no less lavishly appointed. This House was for a long time thought to have a connexion with Tsar Peter the Great who was reputed to have had a Baby House made for him in Holland but refused to accept it in the end, because it was too expensive. It appears, however, that this story was put about by an art dealer in the first half of the nineteenth century, to push up the price for the House. Petronella Oortman, daughter of a maker of rifle barrels from Essen in Germany and of a Dutch mother, was born in 1656. In 1686 she married Jacob Brandt, a native of Fehmarn, an island in the western Baltic. The apparently well-to-do family was able to afford this Baby House which bears Petronella's initials, BO. When her son Jan had to file a petition for bankruptcy in 1743, at a time when the general situation was clearly quite a different one, a Baby House with tortoiseshell inlay was included among the assets.

The Rijksmuseum Baby House is indeed outstanding in being housed in a valuable cabinet with tortoiseshell veneer closely inlaid with arabesques in pewter. A painting by Jacob Appel (1680–1751) shows the House during the early eighteenth century, when long curtains could be drawn in front of the glass doors to protect it. On the ground floor, the relatively narrow kitchen is at the centre. As in the Utrecht House, the hearth is an open one built into the wall. To the left of the kitchen is a large state kitchen where the best china is kept and at the same time displayed, very much as in the Nuremberg Houses. The floor is of marble, and the walls are tiled from top to bottom. The painted-on 'architecture' of the ceiling makes the room appear larger. The walls of the 'tapestry' room on the right are completely covered in hangings embroidered in 'Hungarian flame stitch'. A cabinet lacquered in gold on black displays a collection of shells. At the back, a door leads to the library. As in the Utrecht House, the walls of the reception room on the first floor are completely covered with landscape paintings by Nicolaas Piemont (1644–1709). W. van Rooyen (1650–1723) painted the poultry in a park-like landscape

on the chimney breast, and in the lying-in room opposite the same place is adorned
104 with a painting by J. Voorhout (1647–1723) showing Moses in his basket of rushes. In this room, a bed with velvet hangings is built into a recess, and to the left and right of it are a well-filled linen press and a wardrobe. The walls have been expensively panelled with rosewood, a material also used for the furniture in the reception room. On the second floor is the nursery, with windows in the back wall and between them a large bed with taffeta curtains, a linen room equipped for drying, pressing and ironing, and behind it the maids' room with two beds.

This House, too, contains many quite
101 remarkable items, very fine dishes of Dutch silver, porcelain from East Asia, and glass. The dolls which filled the House with life in the painting by Appel, have unfortunately disappeared.

Margaretha de Ruyter's House

96–98 Since 1924, the Rijksmuseum has had another seventeenth-century House, formerly the property of Mrs van Tienhoven-Hacke[201]. Until recently it was thought to come from the collection of Margaretha Ruyter (died 1689); but actually it belonged to Petronella Dunois and is mentioned among the goods of her dowry when she married the Leyden 'regent' Peter van Groenendijk in 1677. On the ground-floor of this House, the kitchen is flanked by the storeroom with a wine-cellar on the one side, and a sitting-room on the other. In the big lying-in room on the first floor, the walls and the bed with its bunches of red
96 feathers are covered in printed chintz. The ceiling of this room is divided into squares and painted, as the ceiling of the sitting-room besides. As in all Dutch Houses, open fireplaces with tall chimney breasts are used to heat the rooms. The wet-nurse and the maid in the lying-in room, the
97 mistress and the master in the parlour of the first floor, and all the other people in the House wear fashionable garments of the late seventeenth century. On the second floor are a storeroom, the linen room and the nursery.

Sara Ploos van Amstel's House

The two Houses in the Gemeentemuseum at The Hague and the Stedelijk Museum at Haarlem date back to the second quarter of the eighteenth century. These are not doll's cabinets in cupboard form, but regular cupboards, revealing themselves as Baby Houses only when the doors are opened. A broad, solid piece of furniture, the House 105–131 in The Hague[202] accommodates three drawers in its base. The seven pedestals of the much-curved top still hold china bowls, as they did before. Sara Ploos van Amstel had this walnut cupboard made in the autumn 105 of 1743, at a cost of 230 guilders. On 10 April of that year she had at an auction in Amsterdam's Keizerskron acquired three old dolls' cabinets for 903 guilders. She kept very careful records of the things she 25 bought and how everything was set up and arranged, so that we have firsthand information on almost every detail concerning the furnishings. Thus furniture and other objects from the seventeenth century came to be in a House of later design, then as now a very common and natural occurrence in many households and collections.

In this House, too, the most elegant rooms, the music room and the china 110 cabinet, are on the first floor. They have higher ceilings than the others, the height of these rooms being 45cm. The rooms on the ground floor measure 39cm in height, those on the second floor only 37cm. Below, we have the garden at the centre. The owner spent eighteen guilders to have it 114 painted, with vistas opening out in perspective to the sides and back, and with the sky above. The lying-in room on the left came from the third of the cabinets she had acquired, but she added a built-in toilet, and the dolls were given some new clothes and new heads and hands. The kitchen, on the right, comes from the same cabinet; it 119 has been slightly reduced in height, with

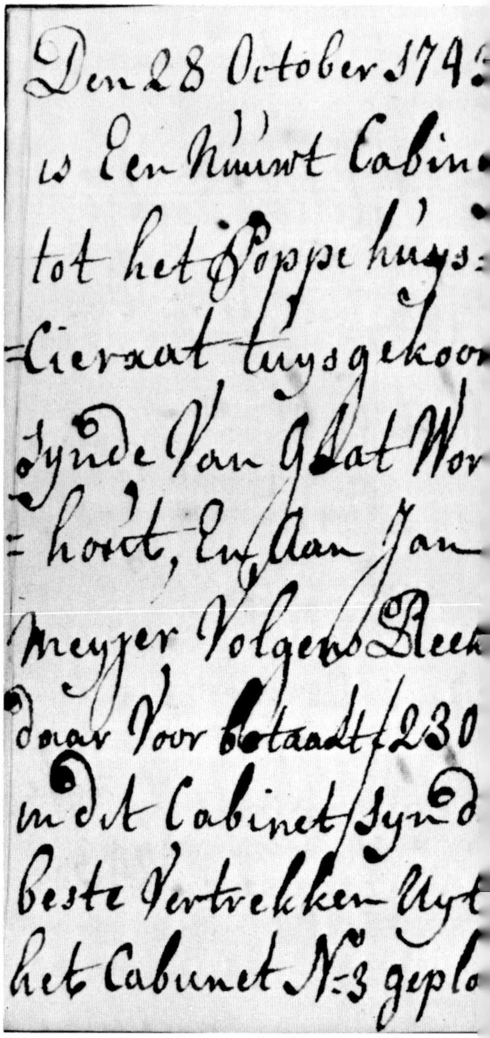
Den 28 October 174
is Een Nieuwt Cabin
tot het Poppe huys:
=Cieraat tuys gekoo
Synde Van Glat Wor
=hout, En Aan Jan
meyer Volgens Reek
daar Voor betaalt f 230
in dit Cabinet Synd
beste Vertrekken Uyt
het Cabinet N:3 geplo

Fig. 25 From the notes made by Sara Ploos van Amstel, concerning the Baby House she was having made.
Den Haag, Gemeentemuseum.

...nt Van de Anderde 230:—
...o Ook de Geschilderde
...n porseleyn kaamer
...t het Cabinet No 2
...de Voornaamste
...en beste & Raarelyxe
...e in de Drie Cabinetten
...weest Syn, die Wy
...11 April 1743
De keysers kroon,
...kogt hadden.

the ceiling repainted. The cupboard standing against the back wall holds pewter plates; Mrs Ploos van Amstel adorned its upper shelf with a lace-edged cloth. Apart from Delftware, she found room in the kitchen for a Japanese porcelain teaset that she had already had for some time; on closer inspection it seems too large in size here. The painted walls of the first floor vestibule imitate plasterwork. The five doors opening from here are of plain wood and unpainted. The narrow strip of carpet was tablet-woven by the owner herself, in a pattern of black and yellow lozenges. The handsome lantern hanging from the ceiling – there is another like it in the Haarlem House – cost her four guilders. Another new acquisition was the clock case with a golden watch inside it. The landscape paintings covering the walls of the music room came from David van der Plaats, the former owner. Two of the six silver sconces in this room were copied to match the other four which came from the second cabinet bought at the auction. Mrs Ploos van Amstel had the harpsichord repainted. Like the books and the viol da gamba, this came from the third cabinet. The dolls and the furniture in the music room she had specially made, but most of the small silver, brass and glass items in that room came from the older cabinets. For the china room she used a small semi-circular display cabinet with glass doors from the second of the doll's cabinets. This was built into the back wall, with eighteen brackets added to the left and right of it, plus four large framed mirrors on the side walls. She paid ten guilders for this. The blue and white ware exhibited in this room are Dutch imitations in opaque glass of the much sought-after Chinese porcelain. Large quantities of this were produced at the time for export to Europe. Imitations in glass of delicately embossed white porcelain – blanc de chine – come partly from the older cabinets, whilst some were added by Mrs Ploos van Amstel.

The four drawers of a seventeenth-century display cabinet completely veneered with tortoiseshell are filled with shells decoratively inlaid in wax. The oval top of a folding table shows delicate lacquer painting in the chinoiserie style of the late seventeenth century. The art and treasure chamber on the second floor contains beautiful furniture of the same period, including a cabinet housing a collection of coins. another with a large collection of shells, and a bookcase. The chaise longue and its cushions are embroidered in the 'Hungarian flame style' popular towards the end of the seventeenth century. The nursery originally also had a cupboard filled with silver toys. It now contains among other items a tester-bed, the edges of its satin curtains charmingly decorated, a high-backed child's chair with early rococo ornaments painted in yellow on a blue ground. Apart from some pieces of baby clothes, here, other garments, this time for adults, many of them beautifully embroidered or trimmed with lace, may be found in the cupboard of the lying-in room and in the plaited baskets of the linen room at the centre of the top floor.

The Baby House from the Blaauw and Rienstra van Stuyvesant Collections

This cabinet, once also belonging to Sara Ploos Van Amstel, later in the Blaauw and Rienstra van Stuyvesant Collections, but now in the Museum at Haarlem[203], even has two sets of doors. The outer door of the cabinet varnished in black is painted in the style of Gérard de Lairesse with representations of Pegasus and the liberal arts, Apollo and the nine Muses. The paintings on the inner doors imitate a stone façade with windows, as if a house had really been built into the cabinet. The rooms of the House occupy four stories. Above the central entrance hall, on the floor above the kitchen and cellars, is a vestibule, and on either side of it the room known as that of the astrologer Ludeman, and the dining room, with silver utensils displayed in the alcove of the back wall. On the second floor are the lying-in room, a parlour with curtains of

55

red moiré before its large windows, and at the centre a room known as the chapel, 132 with an almost circular alcove behind. In this centre room, the walls are painted with fantastic rococo ornaments and with figures in tall niches. On the top floor are the storeroom, a drying attic, and the nursery.

The Gontard House at Frankfurt

This House, similar in many ways to the 136– Dutch Houses and now in the Historical 143 Museum in Frankfurt[204], was formerly in the possession of the von Gontard family in that city. Many changes have been made in this House at different times, and much has 136 been added. The stand and the frame were executed in the nineteenth century. To the 138 left on the ground floor is a storeroom, with the cellar partitioned off by laths at the back. Above this is a stage, now also used for storage. It probably had another purpose originally, for the garden vista painted on the back wall gives the illusion 40 of a wide space. From the central hall, 43 nineteenth-century stairs lead to the upper storey. As in all the other rooms, the floor of the parlour, to the right, is chequered in black and white. The room is heated by an open fire in a voluminous baroque stone 142 fireplace. Above it is the kitchen, where the spaces between the shelves running around the walls are painted with big flowers and foliage. The table-like hearth on the left of the background is quite unique; nothing like it exists in other Southern German or Dutch Baby Houses. The painted ceiling of

the kitchen seems to indicate that the room was formerly used for another purpose. On the landing outside stands a huge linen 141 press. The tiled stove and the cupboard with its carved decorations in the bedroom 139 are from the seventeenth century. The Gontard House provides particularly good documentation of how the different purposes which a Baby House served in the course of two hundred years have left their traces, with many changes made particularly during the nineteenth century.

The lying-in room

In every one of the Dutch Houses still in 89, existence and also in some of the English 96, Houses, the lying-in room occupies a 103, prominent place. Considerable importance 114, attached to such lying-in rooms, witness 148 the information given by Gédéon Tallemant de Réaux (1619–92), and passed on by Henry René d'Allemagne[205], that Cardinal Richelieu (1585–1642) had presented the Duchess of Enghien with a lying-in room, with dolls that could be dressed and undressed. The museums at Strasbourg and Frankfurt-on-Main[206] have dolls' rooms of obviously Alsatian origin, 206– with clay-figures dating back to the late 207 eighteenth century, and these are either lying-in rooms, or they show the christening celebrated beside the mother's bed. Here we have evidence that a custom originally known in court and upper middle-class circles, as shown by Richelieu's lying-in room and those to be found in Baby Houses, later became a popular tradition.

Dolls' Houses of the Eighteenth Century

England

A third Baby House in the Rijksmuseum at Amsterdam that dates back to the middle of the eighteenth century, is in a style similar to that of the eighteenth-century English Houses, an actual house, with three stories rising above a low basement and an outdoor staircase leading to the front door[207]. Sparsely furnished nowadays, the Amsterdam House has 26 windows and two doors in its pilastered façade, eight windows in each side wall, a side entrance instead of one on the right side.

The oldest English House still in existence originally belonged to Ann Sharp, born in 1691, a daughter of John Sharp, Archbishop of York. It was given to her by her godmother, the then Princess Anne[208]. It is actually a cupboard housing four floors with rooms that are filled with a great variety of things. It was not until after 1700 that English Baby Houses developed into actual houses, with a front that opened and closed, usually on a tall stand. The Westbrook Baby House[209] is said to have been a parting gift made for Elizabeth, the young daughter of John Westbrook of Essex, in 1705, when the family were leaving the Isle of Dogs. It probably is a miniature replica of the house they had lived in. Another house dated 1709, with a gabled façade consisting of three 'parts', now at the Bethnal Green Museum, turns out not to be a house at all, but opens up to reveal a child's wardrobe[210].

161

A particularly magnificent Baby House still stands at Uppark in Sussex[211]. Here is a typical Great House in the Palladian style, with three stories above five pillared arcades. Seven joyful genii adorn the balustrade at the top of the house, and the central gable bears the arms of the Fetherstonhaugh family. The house once belonged to Sarah, daughter of Christopher Lethieullier, who married Matthew Fetherstonhaugh in 1747, when he had just acquired Uppark. The rooms on the lower floor – a hall, with the stairs leading to the floor above, the kitchen and one room –

145–
149

149

have lower ceilings than those of the main storey, and those of the top floor which are not quite as high as the latter. All the rooms are panelled in white. Again there is a lying-in room, beside the dining room with its many pieces of silverware at the centre of the first floor. Each of the three rooms on the top floor contains a curtained tester-bed, but here one misses the dolls – wax heads for the family, wooden heads for the servants – that fill the rooms below with life.

145/
146

A very similar exterior is presented by a Baby House of approximately the same period at Nostell Priory near Wakefield in Yorkshire[212], still in the possession of the Winn family, who started to build a new Great House there in 1733. It is said that Thomas Chippendale had a hand in making the furniture for this Baby House. Chippendale was born quite near to Nostell Priory, in 1718, and created a number of pieces of furniture in oak and other native woods there, before moving to London in the 1740s. A special feature of the Uppark House is that each of its nine rooms has its own door that may be opened, in the façade. The front of the Nostell Priory House consists of two tall wings that open. As in Uppark, the entrance hall at the centre of the lower floor has the staircase going up the wall at the back. Except for the kitchen, the walls are either panelled, painted or covered in a Chinese wallpaper. The long curtains of the beds and side windows are of velvet, silk moiré, or flowered chintz. The family arms on the gable bear the date 1743.

Another, smaller, house of that period is the Blackett Baby House in the Museum of London[213]. As with the late House at Amsterdam, a symmetrical double flight of outside stairs leads straight up to the first floor. The façade has two wings that open to reveal two rooms one above the other, first and second floor, on either side. It has four sash-windows that can be pushed up. An outstanding feature of the Blackett House are the painted wallpapers in three of its rooms. The kitchen has an open

157–
159

159

fireplace of the type also seen in the Dutch Baby Houses. The Tate House in the Bethnal Green Museum[214] has double balustraded stairs elegantly curving upwards to its front door on the first floor. It was made in Dorset in about 1760, in the style of that period, furnished during the last third of that century, and redecorated in about 1830.

150–
152
156

In England even the early Baby Houses were gifts given to small girls who may well have played with them. Thus they were neither object lessons like the German Houses, nor cabinet pieces made for display like the Dutch ones. Their furnishings and fittings therefore are not as rich and varied as those of the Houses of Continental Europe, nor do they hold the same interest for social historians. It is not surprising, then, that the earliest document Vivien Greene has been able to reproduce is a trade-card published on 14 December 1762 by a toyseller named Bellamy 'At the Green Parrot, near Chancery Lane, Holborn'[215]. This announces, among other things, 'Fine Babies and Baby-Houses, with all Sorts of Furniture at the lowest Price', an indication that at that period Baby Houses were not only made to order, but also for general sale, so that there must have been some serial production. It also provides evidence that children must have actually played with such Houses, probably even quite extensively.

Sweden and Italy

A Swedish Baby House dating back to about 1740 is in the Nordiska Museet at Stockholm[216]. It is built into a cabinet on slender curved legs, with a glass front and angled sides, also of glass. This really no longer has the air of a genuine house and home, however. The four compartments of the cabinet each display the furniture for one room, with a kind of ballroom at the top. I would describe this as a cabinet showing domestic furniture rather than a house built into a cabinet.

The Bologna House[217] is in a class by itself. It has the appearance of a single-storey eighteenth-century Italian Palazzo. One can walk around it and look in from all sides through the large windows which can also be opened. The furniture and fittings are so sumptuous and elegant that one wonders if this was not a model, rather than a collector's piece, an object lesson, or a toy.

164–
168

'Mon Plaisir' at Arnstadt

Oddly enough, no large dolls' houses from the eighteenth century are kept in Germany. Was no one interested in creating new ones, at a time when such houses had not yet become children's toys? One would almost assume this to be the case, particularly as *Mon Plaisir*, the dolls' town owned by Princess Augusta Dorothea von Schwarzburg, once again represents a miniature world created by and for adults, this time a small town in Thuringia, residence of a princely family.

169–
191

The princess had come from Brunswick-Wolfenbüttel to Arnstadt in 1684, when she was eighteen. In 1697, the counts of Schwarzburg were elevated to the rank of princes. The prince, Anton Günther II, died in 1716, the princess not until 1751, after 35 years of widowhood. She was a passionate collector, getting heavily in debt quite early on, and with her court and the assistance of numerous craftsmen whose names have not come down to us, she created the dolls' town, starting in 1704 if not before. The town consists of 82 units. Most of them are not really houses, but boxes of various sizes, some placed on top of each other, connected by stairs and provided with a roof. Two rows of boxes represent the weekly market. There are numerous stands, with flaps to close them up for the night, where goods are for sale. Ordinary townspeople and the more well-to-do are examining and buying the wares. There are copper and brass utensils, a hatter and a shoemaker, a wax-chandler, and next to him a knife-grinder with his tools.

170

The vegetable woman is sitting in front of a table filled with garden produce. A tradeswoman has pottery ware for sale spread on the ground around her. One man is pushing a wheelbarrow, another leading a horse that is pulling a loaded sled. A picture-seller is there, also a country girl carrying a large basket on her back. The 171– tradesmen's houses are those of the baker, 175 the butcher, the cooper, the cabinetmaker, the turner and the weaver, and the apothecary is there as well, with a well-equipped dispensary. Often the wife is helping the husband with his work. The small farm has a farmhouse made of brick below, and half-timbered above. The farmer's wife is looking after the poultry, the farmer after 176 the animals in the stable, whilst the young people, with the baby in the cradle beside them, are at breakfast, and a maid is making butter. The nursery in a commoner's 182 house is different from the princely one, and life is altogether more stylish in the prince's residence. There, coaches drawn 177 by two or four horses are arriving, and the princess is just alighting from a sedan- 179 chair. The cellarer is busy in the wine cellar, and the cook in the kitchen, assisted by maids and kitchen boys. The house- 180 keeper, recognizable from the two great keys attached to her belt, is at work in the linen room, with a maid. Two chamber- 183 maids are making the bed, a tester-bed with its tall headboard decorated with a picture of a flower-vase in an oval car- touche. In the nursery, a servant is taking 184 an infant in its swaddling clothes to the

princess. The cradle and basket for the baby are beautifully plaited. In other rooms one sees a lady at her toilet assisted by two maids, the court hairdresser at his morning tasks, ladies playing board games, drinking 190 tea and coffee, parties engaged in card 178, games and music-making, gentlemen 188 smoking, and the steward making his daily 189 report. 187

Each room is furnished in a distinct style, usually in the most excellent taste. There are built-in and tiled fireplaces, silk hangings on the walls, draped curtains, coloured wallpapers and others of pressed and gilded leather, pictures and mirrors and many different items of furniture, de- signed for all kinds of purposes, as well as all the necessary utensils and implements. The china cabinet is particularly lavishly 186 furnished; its numerous precious vases on their curved brackets are reflected in the gold-framed wall-mirrors. The princess's cabinet of art works and curiosities has not been forgotten, nor the cabinet of the court historiographer, or the garden, very formal in the French style, and finally the court theatre. There are also scenes from the Ursuline Convent at Erfurt, for the prin- 191 cess had become a convert to Catholicism; hence also the baroque church, where Mass is being celebrated. The numerous dolls with their delicately modelled wax heads are dressed in accordance with their station in life, in the style of the period. The dolls' town of *Mon Plaisir* – largely forgotten during the nineteenth century – continues to be a great attraction to this day.

Beginning in the year 1793, the Nuremberg merchant Georg Hieronymus Bestelmeyer[219] issued a total of nine instalments of his extraordinarily wide-ranging catalogue of toys of all kinds. Every piece was fully described, and illustrated with a tiny copperplate engraving. In one of its later instalments, this earliest catalogue of **26** toys offers a nicely furnished dolls' house, in two sizes (Nos. 815 and 835), and also separate rooms, kitchens, and above all toy shops. The description of the house includes the following words: 'that children may arrange the furniture inside and play with it'. Referring to a kitchen, No. 197, Bestelmeyer stated quite emphatically that this was a 'new kind of play-kitchen'; 'it is much more life-like than those commonly known heretofore, having a roof with a chimney, a large door, and two glass windows.' No. 690 on the other hand – farmhouse room, reception room, lying-in room, masque room, picture gallery – consisted of rooms cut out from cardboard, to be put together. Individual items of furniture were listed, for instance a wardrobe filled with clothes (No. 540), a food or glass cabinet (No. 541), whilst No. 542 was a salon or ballroom that could be folded up, with furniture. Toyshops clearly predominated: No. 145b, a 'grocer's shop, wooden, painted, with numerous drawers and two glass doors; No. 243, a shop selling pewter ware, with two movable figures, 'in the same manner are obtainable also grocer's and apothecary's shops'; No. 301, a raffling shop with contents; No. 357, a fashion shop with a boutique in green lacquer paint, and in it, gowns, cloaks, hats, purses; No. 425, a shop selling pewter ware that can be opened and shut, with assorted pewter ware and a figure; No. 564, a merchant's shop with all kinds of groceries and an office attached; No. 565, a merchant's shop with similar contents (e.g. sugar and tobacco, in drawers, jars, tubs), also with an office; No. 582, a shop selling toys, in it 'most of the things that are in the line of playthings', including a tinsel angel, six-

teen pieces and a woman, altogether.

Shops

Two of the seventeenth-century Nuremberg Baby Houses still in existence, the one dated 1639 and the one formerly owned by **18,** the Bäumler family, have a 'merchant's **44** shop' in the basement. The first of these also serves as an office, to judge by the furnishings. From the seventeenth century onwards, shops and storage vaults could be part of the Nuremberg Houses. Shops, with their contents designed to change hands, really ask to be played with, and so it is easy to understand why in Germany they were the first part of a house – apart perhaps from the kitchen, where dishes and utensils also ask to be handled – to be made into playthings, where children could trade **27** in all kinds of goods, move them about, display and sell them, and thus enjoy them in play and occupy their time with them. The oldest separate toyshop known to us, probably dating back to the middle of the eighteenth century (in the Germanisches **208–** Nationalmuseum at Nuremberg) is to be **214** looked at only, and this probably not for mere reasons of accidentally being preserved. Extremely plain on the outside, it is a small wooden box, with paper stars pasted on it; opened up, it consists of one shop with a male shopkeeper above and another with a woman below. The goods are merely small blocks of wood affixed to the shelves, painted in various colours to indicate what they are supposed to be: a picture of a shop, therefore, not something one can play with. The rather larger grocer's shop at the Schweizerischen **212–** Landesmuseum in Zurich is also a box, **213** albeit with flowers painted on it. It, too, offers no 'real' goods, but at least the 'sugar loaves' hanging from the ceiling look like sugar loaves, one can pick them up and play with them as if they were real, and there are real jars, sacks, drawers, and even a pair of scales. Not much later, most of the goods in Bestelmeyer's shops probably were 'real'. Fashion and milliners' shops, one of

Dolls' Houses as Playthings

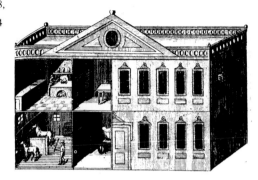

Fig. 26 Dolls' house. Copper engraving from *Pädagogisches Magazin . . .* issued by Georg Hieronymus Bestelmeyer. Nuremberg, 1793 ff.

Fig. 28 Shop selling glass wares. Lithograph from a Nuremberg toy catalogue, second quarter of nineteenth century.

Fig. 27 Two girls with dolls' kitchen. Coloured engraving, fourth quarter of eighteenth century.

which is listed in his catalogue, became particularly popular during the Biedermeier period. Today they provide us with a treasure trove of lovely things. Their contents seem to have been fashioned, collected and arranged with really loving care. Not only are there hats, caps, veils, and shawls for sale, but also complete gowns with all accessories, such as jabots, collars, cuffs and belts, stays, bags and purses, fans, gloves and coloured ribbons. Other items on offer are embroidered bell-pulls and cushion-fronts, charmingly decorated braces and suspenders, excellently starched collars and shirt-fronts for the young cavalier. Everything is put away neatly in cupboards and drawers, on cap-stands and clothes-hangers. Then there are silk threads in a wide range of colours, needles, pearls, hooks and eyes, buttons and buckles and everything else that may be needed by the milliner, the dressmaker, or the housewife doing her own sewing.

It was indeed with shops like these that play began. There they were, waiting for their young customers to flock to them, to delve and pick and choose, to try on and to buy. Soon bakeries, butchers' shops, and others selling basketware, glasses and even toys, made their appearance. Next came coach houses with carriages and sleighs, stables with draught and saddle-horses, laundries and poultry yards. These and other items of the kind were from the early nineteenth century onwards offered in toy catalogues, many of them printed in colour, and it is from these catalogues that we know those shops almost better than from the few examples that are still in existence.

Rooms and houses

During the same period, Baby Houses and dolls' rooms also became playthings. Now they were no longer for display, and the completeness of the household that was the aim with their object-lesson predecessors, ceased to be. In becoming playthings they became more one-sided, losing that dimension which previously had made them into the image of a domestic world complete in itself. The Baby Houses of the seventeenth and also the early eighteenth century reflected such a world; the dolls' houses made for play in the nineteenth century are limited to certain aspects. With individual items becoming more and more realistic – Bestelmeyer boasts 'running water' in his toy kitchen No. 1012, 'children take great pleasure in this' – the former abundance is lost. In the Baby Houses of the seventeenth century it seems that nothing has been forgotten, and they stimulate most of all the informed imagination of adult viewers, letting individual details as well as the whole house come very much to life. The dolls' houses and rooms of a more recent date are mostly intended for children, and need to be 'handled' for a relationship to be established. They are brought to life only by the child playing with them. The former nature of the thing has become subject to limitation, but with the limits set by their being destined for toys, the dolls' houses of the nineteenth century – and also separate rooms as independent units – are able to give the child the stimulus it needs to make the house its own in play. They were sufficiently realistic to involve the child's fantasy, indeed to evoke it, and yet not so perfect that there was no room for the child to develop its own ideas. On the other hand they were not so over-elaborate that they provided no scope for play – meaning over and above all the development of creative imagination. Real children's play means bringing objects to life, interpreting them and reading things into them in sheer endless imagining. Childhood play certainly is anything but having to try to find something with which to while away the time, anything but mere occupation to get through the hours and days[221]. Proper play was also what the nineteenth-century dolls' houses were for. They were less ambitious than their predecessors, for the very reason that they were now designed for children, to be their playthings.

The furniture and other items found in

those dolls' houses followed the fashions of the times: Biedermeier, Second Rococo, Historism with the Neo-renaissance or what was called the Old German style, Neo-baroque, Art Nouveau, Neo-classicism, and Modern Functionalism. Some are perfect miniature replicas, others bear only a superficial resemblance to the originals. As in the old Bestelmeyer catalogues, cardboard imitations were available of furniture and indeed whole rooms and even houses. Lamps and flower-stands as well as pieces of furniture were also cast in pewter.

Epilogue

These toy dolls' houses and dolls' rooms have for a long time been objects for enthusiasm among adult admirers and collectors, who often do not hesitate to complement various old pieces with others, making up deficiencies as they think fit, and finally producing a completely new ensemble. They are thus putting their own individual stamp on their dolls' world, often identifying with it almost completely, and this may of course have a certain charm. One has to be careful, however, not to include such 'sets of furnishings' among the ranks of Baby Houses with genuine furnishings, whether entirely original or assembled over a number of generations.

In England, where the oldest of the Baby Houses still in existence were designed for small girls, their furnishings do not show the abundance and completeness of detail of the Southern German and Dutch Baby Houses. During the nineteenth century, some English ladies would commission Baby Houses to be made and furnished according to their personal taste. In about the year 1860, Mrs Bryant of Oakenshaw[222] had such a House made. It has a kitchen and a sitting-room on the ground floor, a large sitting-room on the first and two bedrooms on the second floor (Bethnal Green-Museum). Did Mrs Bryant perhaps have her own house copied for this, as a number of eighteenth-century English Baby Houses reflect the architecture of their owners' homes? An almost extreme case in point is Queen Mary's Dolls' House at Windsor Castle, a perfect piece of work, now a great tourist attraction, that was created in the early Twenties of the present century[223]. Could one call it a late successor, in our age of Perfectionism, of the Baby Houses from the seventeenth and the Arnstadt dolls' town from the early eighteenth century? Something quite different is Titania's Palace[224], a miniature dream palace which Sir Nevile Wilkinson had had made between 1907 and 1922 and which then travelled all around the world for many years, on display to collect money for good causes. It was sold by auction for the first time at Christie's in 1967. When it came up for auction again in 1978, it went for an unbelievably high sum of money, demonstrating once again the high price that may be put on dreams and fantasy.

275–278

Fig. 29   Two milliner's shops. Lithographs from a Nuremberg toy catalogue, second quarter of nineteenth century.

Appendices

Notes

[1] Jacob Stockbauer, 'Das Dockenhaus in der Kunstkammer Herzog Albrechts V. von Bayern,' in *Anz. f. Kunde der dt. Vorzeit* n.s. 26 (1879): cols. 313–20; Otto Hartig, 'Münchner Kunstler und Kunstsachen 2: 1520–1559,' in *Munchn. Jb.* n.s. 7 (1930): 370/71; L. Bayer : 8–22, 7 Note 50.

[2] Alexander von Reitzenstein, *Die alte bayerische Stadt in den Modellen des Drechslermeisters Jacob Sandtner* (Munich, 1967).

[3] Cf. the inventory made in 1596, after the death of Archduke Ferdinand, in *Jb. d. kunsthist. Slgn. d. Allerh. Kaiserhauses* 7 (1888): CXXVI–CCCXII; 10 (1889): I–X.

[4] Norbert Elias, *Über den Prozess der Zivilisation. Soziogenetische und psychogenetische Untersuchungen I. Wandlungen des Verhaltens in den weltlichen Oberschichten des Abendlandes,* 2nd ed. (Bern, 1969): 239/40.

[5] Munich, Bayer. Staatsbibl. cod. germ. 2133, No. 2150 – 2228.

[6] Oscar Doering, 'Philipp Hainshofers Beschreibung des sogenannten pommerschen Meierhofes,' in *Zs. d. Hist. Ver. f. Schwaben u.* Neuburg 18 (1891): 67–86; Julius Lessing and Adolf Brüning, *Der Pommersche Kunstschrank* (Berlin, 1905): 56–68; L. Bayer : 23–31.

[7] Whilst L. Bayer (pp. 8–22) has made the descriptions given in the Inventory into a tour of the House, with her interpretations, I have adhered strictly to the details given by Fickler; I have corrected a few factual errors by L. Bayer.

[8] *Wörterbüchlein zum Nutz und Ergötzen der Schuljugend,* 2nd ed. (Nuremberg, 1733): 52. Every word is accompanied by a woodcut illustration in this book.

[9] Cf. J. Lessing and A. Brüning (Note 6): 47, plate XXXVI.

[10] Theodor Distel, 'Spielsachen für die Kinder des Kurfürsten August von Sachsen,' in *Anz. d.f. Kunde d. dt. Vorzeit* n.s.28 (1881): cols. 49–51.

[11] J. Lessing and A. Brüning (Note 6): 64–66.

[12] 'Modernized' quote from Jacob and Wilhelm Grimm, *Deutsches Wörterbuch* 7 (1889): col. 2247.

[13] Johann Heinrich Zeller, *Grosses, vollständiges Universal – Lexicon* 23 (Leipzig, 1741): col. 1634.

[14] Archiv des Germanischen Nationalmuseums Nuremberg (referred to as GNM).

[15] GNM. Inv. No. HB 2243 and HB 24762. L.v. Wilckens: p. 5/6; I did not at that time take into account the fact that Anna Köferlin used the small foot measure; because of this, the measurements given now are somewhat smaller; L. Bayer: 32–34. I am greatly indebted to Frau B. Richter, Landeskirchliches Archiv, Nuremberg who compiled the biographical data for Anna Köferlin and her family which had been previously unknown. In the poem, necessary additions and explanations are given in brackets.

[16] Georg Kaspar Nägler, *Die Monogrammisten* 3 (Munich, 1863): No. 1181.

[17] Alfred Sitte, 'Aus den Inventarien des Schlosses zu Pottendorf,' in *Berichte u. Mitt d. Alterthumsver. zu Wien* 40 (1906): 119 ff., esp. 126.

[18] Paul von Stetten, *Erläuterungen der in Kupfer gestochenen Vorstellungen aus der Geschichte der Stadt Augsburg* (Augsburg, 1765): 163.

[19] Hans Boesch, 'Die Puppenhäuser des Germanischen Museums,' in *Anz.f.Kunde d. dt. Vorzeit* n.s. 26 (1879) col. 233.

[20] L. v. Wilckens 'Ein Modelbuch von 1517 aus dem Nürnberger Clarenkloster,' in *Anz. d. GNM* (1967): 27–29; another hand-written pattern book is in the possession of Heidelberg University Library, pal. germ. 551.

[21] Theodor Volbehr, *Ein Puppenhaus. Kaiser–Friedrich–Museum Magdeburg, Museum Booklet No.* 9 (Magdeburg, n.d.); L. Bayer: 59.

[22] Inv. No. W 41–1922 *Dolls and Dolls' houses. Victoria and Albert Museum Small Picture Book No.* 16 (London, 1950): Fig.18; L. Bayer: 54–57; J. Latham: 33/34; E. King: 148 (picture of the façade).

[23] K. Gröber: Fig. 35, Plate IV; Hermann Schmitz, *Deutsche Möbel des Barock und Rokoko* (Stuttgart, 1923): Fig. p. VIII/IX; L. Bayer: 51–53.

[24] K. Gröber: Figs. 37, 67, 77; L. Bayer: 63–65.

[25] Meta la Roche, *Spielsachen im alten Basel* (Basle, 1958): 20/21; L. Bayer: 76/77.

[26] L. Bayer: 73–76.

[27] Cf. L. Bayer: 42, and Note 161/62. I would stress, however, that the Sadeler engraving must have been known to the artist who painted the picture in the Baby House.

[28] H. Boesch (Note 19): cols. 232/33.

[29] Cf. Note 14.

[30] *Die so kluge als künstliche von Arachne und Penelope getreulich unterwiesene Hauss-Halterin* Nuremberg (1703): 192/93.

[31] Georg Steinhausen, ed., *Briefwechsel Balthasar Baumgartners des Jüngeren mit Magdalena geb. Behaim,* Bibliothek des Literarischen Vereins Stuttgart No. 204 (Tübingen, 1895): 84.

[32] Haushaltungsbuch des Georg Friedrich Behaim. Behaim–Archiv, Deposited in the Archives of the GNM.

[33] About 1420, Winterthur, Dr Oskar Reinhart's collection; Georg Schmidt and Anna Maria Cetto, *Schweizer Malerei und Zeichnung im 15. und 16. Jahrhundert* (Frankfurt–on–Main, n.d.): Plate I, p. III; About 1460, Basle, Öffentliche Kunstsammlung; ibid. Plate 28, p. XVIII.

[34] Ludwig Grote, 'Die 'Vorderstube' des Sebald Schreyer. Ein Beitrag zur Rezeption der Renaissance in Nürnberg', in *Anz. d. GNM* (1954–59) : 43–67, esp. 57/58.

[35] 'Aussteuer der Anna Kress' (1503–28) im Kress–Archiv, deposited in the Archives of the GNM.

[36] Edmund Ungerer, ed., *Elsässische Altertümer in Burg und Haus, in Kloster und Kirche* 2 (Strasbourg, 1917): 103.

[37] Haushaltungsbuch des Paulus Behaim, Behaim Archives, deposited in the Archives of the GNM, most of it published in *Mitt. d. Ver. f. Gesch. d. Stadt Nürnberg* 7 (1888): 57 ff. Re 'schetter', cf. p. 48/49.

[38] *Mitt. d. Ver. F. Gesch. d. Stadt Nürnberg* 7 (1888): 152.

[39] E. Ungerer (Note 36), 1 (1913): 127.

[40] Karen Stolleis, *Die Gewänder aus der Lauinger Fürstengruft, Forschungshefte* 3 (Bayer. Nationalmuseum, München & Berlin, 1977): 158.

[41] Karl Bräuer, *Studien zur Geschichte der Lebenshaltung in Frankfurt/M. während des 17. und 18. Jahrhunderts* 2 (Frankfurt/M., 1915): 50.

[42] *Mitt. d. Ver. f. Gesch. d. Stadt Nürnberg* 7 (1888): 141.

[43] GNM, Inv. No. HB 3095–97; L. v. Wilckens, Plate II–VIII; the third sheet (not shown) depicts a section through the second storey.

[44] Cf. Note 30, here p. 215/16.

[45] L. Grote (Note 34): 44.

[46] Cf. Note 30, here p. 190.

[47] L. Grote (Note 34): 45 ff.

[48] *Mitt. d. Ver. f. Gesch. d. Stadt Nürnberg* 7 (1888): 79.

[49] Ibid. : 140.

[50] Ibid. : 152.

[51] Ibid. : 141/42.

[52] Cf. Note 32.

[53] In the Löffelholz Archives, deposited in the Archives of the GNM.

[54] Cf. Note 30, here p. 191.

[55] Ibid. : 193/94.

[56] *Luisa Hager, Alter Wandbespannungen und Tapeten* (Darmstadt, 1954); Heinrich Olligs, ed., *Tapeten, Ihre Geschichte bis zur Gegenwart,* 3 vols. (Braunschweig, 1970).

[57] Cf. Note 43; L. v. Wilckens, Plate VI.

[58] *Mitt. d. Ver f. Gesch. d. Stadt Nürnberg* 7 (1888): 41–43.

[59] K. Bräuer (Note 41); 1: 172–87.

[60] Monika Heffels, *Die deutschen Handzeichnungen des 18. Jahrhunderts,* Kataloge des Germanischen Nationalmuseums (Nuremberg, 1969): 349–58 Cat. No. 427–40, esp. 432, 434, 437.

[61] Munich, Staatl. Graph. Slg. Inv. No. 118321; L. v. Wilckens, Plate I; Dieter Kuhrmann, *Die Frühzeit des Holzschnitts,* exhib. (Munich, 1970) Cat. No. 81.

[62] Theodor Hampe, *Gedichte vom Hausrat aus dem 15. und 16. Jahrhundert,* Facsimile edition (Strasbourg, 1899).

[63] Ibid.

[64] J. and W. Grimm (Note 12) 10, 1 (Leipzig 1905): cols. 1892/93.

[65] E. Ungerer (Note 36): 100/01.

[66] E. Ungerer (Note 39): 169.

[67] Ibid. : 112–14.

[68] In the Imhoff Archives, deposited in the Archives of the GNM.

[69] A. F. Butsch, 'Inventar einer Fuggerschen Hauseinrichtung', in *Zs. d. Hist. Ver f. Schwaben u. Neuburg* 1 (1974): 122–31.

[70] C. Reichardt, 'Ein bürgerlicher Haushalt im Jahre 1612 eines Wildunger Bürgers im Archiv von Niederwildungen', in *Zs. f. Kulturgesch.* 8 (1901): 195–217.

[71] G. Steinhausen (Note 31): 244/45.

[72] Ibid.: 65/66.

[73] Cf. Note 14.

[74] In the Löffelholz Archives, deposited in the Archives of the GNM.

[75] In the Archives of the GNM.

[76] Cf. Note 53.

[77] Cf. Note 30, here p. 182/83.

[78] E. Ungerer (Note 39): 112.

[79] Cf Note 68.

[80] E. Ungerer (Note 39): 54–57.

[81] Friedrich Schneider, *Ein Mainzer Domherr der erzstiftlichen Zeit. Wennemar von Bodelschwingh 1558–1605. Leben, Haus und Habe* (Freiburg i. Br., 1907): 167.

[82] In the Archives of the GNM.

[83] Cf. Note 30, here p. 189/90.

[84] Cf. Note 68.

[85] L. Gerbing, 'Ein Schlossinventar des 17. Jahrhunderts', in *Zs. f. Kulturgesch.* 4 (1897): 198–212.

[86] J. and W. Grimm (Note 12); 11, 1, I(1935): col. 469.

[87] Karl Goedeke, ed., *Johannes Römoldt* (Hanover, 1855): 42, verses 1234–40.

[88] A. Mörath, 'Das Inventar eines Würzburger Domherrnhofes vom Jahre 1557', in *Anz. f. Kunde d. dt. Vorzeit* n.s. 27 (1880): cols. 33–38, esp. 34.

[89] F. Schneider (Note 81): 174, 177.

[90] Cf. Note 14.

[91] Cf. Note 62.

[92] In the Imhoff Archives, deposited in the Archives of the GNM.

[93] In the Behaim Archives, deposited in the Archives of the GNM.

[94] Cf. Note 53.

[95] *Mitt. d. Ver. f. Gesch. d. Stadt Nürnberg* 7 (1888): 52.

[96] L. v. Wilckens, 'Die textilen Schätze der Lorenzkirche', in *500 Jahre Hallenchor St. Lorenz. Nürnberger Forschungen* 20 (Nuremberg, 1977): 152.

[97] L. v. Wilckens, 'Textilien', in *Bayern, Kunst und Kultur*, exhib. (Munich 1972): 196.

[98] E. Ungerer (Note 36): 149, 151.

[99] K. Bräuer (Note 59): 160.

[100] Cf. Note 68.

[101] K. Bräuer (Note 41): 46.

[102] E. Ungerer (Note 36): 34.

[103] A. F. Butsch (Note 69): 130.

[104] Cf. Note 14.

[105] Lindsay Boynton, ed., *The Hardwick Hall Inventories of 1601* (London, 1971): 37–40.

[106] F. Schneider (Note 81): 167.

[107] Peter Strieder, *Deutsche Malerei nach Dürer* (Königstein/Ts., 1966): col. plate on p. 62.

[108] Günther Schiedlausky, *Essen und Trinken, Tafelsitten bis zum Ausgang des Mittelalters* (Munich, 1956): Plate 43, top.

[109] Alfons Ott, *Tausend Jahre Musikleben 800–1800* (Munich, 1961): col. plate IV, Plate 50.

[110] L. Gerbing (Note 85): 199, 208.

[111] Cf. Note 68.

[112] A. Ott (Note 109): Plate 48.

[113] L. v. Wilckens: Fig. p. 47.

[114] Brigitte Volk-Knüttel, *Wandteppiche für den Münchner Hof nach Entwürfen von Peter Candid. Forschungshefte* 2, ed. Bayer, Nationalmuseum (Munich & Berlin, 1976): col. plate 6, Plate 144/45.

[115] E. Ungerer (Note 39): 125.

[116] E. Ungerer (Note 36): 150.

[117] (Note 105): passim.

[118] Cf. Note 32.

[119] In the Archives of the GNM.

[120] E. Ungerer (Note 36): 76.

[121] George Himmelheber, 'Zweigeschossige Schränke der Spätgotik in Oberdeutschland', in *Münchn. Jb.* 3 F. 18 (1967): 98, 109 Note 2.

[122] M. Heffels (Note 60): 356–58 Cat. No. 439.

[123] Cf. Note 30, here p. 196.

[124] E. Ungerer (Note 36): 156.

[125] L. Gerbing (Note 85): 198, 202.

[126] Cf. Note 93.

[127] E. Ungerer (Note 36): 149, 151.

[128] Cf. Note 93.

[129] B. Volk-Knüttel (Note 114): Plate 145.

[130] K. Bräuer (Note 41): 49.

[131] E. Ungerer (Note 39): 173, 162.

[132] L. v. Wilckens: Plate III; cf. also Note 37.

[133] Cf. Note 14.

[134] L. Gerbing (Note 85): 198–212.

[135] Last of all: *1471 Albrecht Dürer 1971*. Exhib. (Nuremberg, 1971): 382 Cat. No. 708/09; Germanisches Nationalmuseum, *Führer durch die Sammlungen* (Munich, 1977): 87 No. 217 with col. illustr.

[136] A. Mörath (Note 88): col. 35.

[137] *Mitt. d. Ver. f. Gesch. d. Stadt Nürnberg* 7 (1888): 40–42.

[138] Wilhelm Loose, ed., *Anton Tuchers Haushaltbuch 1507 –17. Bibliothek des Literarischen Vereins Stuttgart* 134 (Tübingen, 1877): 58, 67, 96, 140, 154, 156.

[139] *Wörterbüchlein* (Note 8): 59/60.

[140] Emil Major, 'Der Basler Hausrat im Zeitalter der Spätgotik', in *Basler Jb.* (1911): 241–315, esp. 261.

[141] E. Ungerer (Note 39): 87.

[142] K. Bräuer (Note 41): 66–68.

[143] *Mitt. d. Ver. f. Gesch. d. Stadt Nürnberg* 7 (1888): 71.

[144] *Inv. No. Gm 1463. Führer* (Note 135): 76 No. 186 m. Fig.

[145] Cf. Note 30, here p. 202.

[146] Cf. Note 32.

[147] Cf. Note 30, here p. 202.

[148] K. Bräuer (Note 59): 175–78.

[149] E. Ungerer (Note 39): 115/16.

[150] Friedrich Bothe 'Frankfurter Patriziervermögen im 16. Jahrhundert', *Archiv für Kulturgeschichte*, 2nd supplement (Berlin, 1908): 32–34; idem; 'Stein– und Tonmodel als Kuchenformen', in *Rep. f. Kunstwiss.* 43 (1922): 80–92; finally also Fritz Arens, 'Die ursprüngliche Verwendung gotischer Stein– und Tonmodel', in *Mainzer Zs* 66 (1971) 106–31, with further lit. and list of moulds to be found in Middle–Rhine museums.

[151] Cf. Note 74.

[152] In the Kress Archives, deposited in the Archives of the GNM.

[153] *Mitt. d. Ver. f. Gesch. d. Stadt Nürnberg* 7 (1888): 40–42.

[154] Cf. Note 68.

[155] K. Bräuer (Note 41): 135.

[156] *Mitt. d. Ver. f. Gesch. d. Stadt Nürnberg* 7 (1888): 42.

[157] W. Loose (Note 138), e.g. pp. 33, 35.

[158] *Mitt. d. Ver. f. Gesch. d. Stadt Nürnberg* 7 (1888): 100.

[159] Cf. Note 30, here pp. 483–86; *Schauplatz der Künste und Handwerke* 16 (Berlin, 1788): 197–202.

[160] Cf. Note 68.

[161] C. Reichardt (Note 70): 202.

[162] Th. Hampe (Note 62).

[163] Cf. Note 30, here p. 203.

[164] *Ibid., p. 205.*

[165] K. Bräuer (Note 59): 199–211.

[166] *Haushaltungsbuch des Christoph Kress.* Kress Archives, deposited in the Archives of the GNM.

[167] Cf. Note 32.

[168] *Haushaltungsbuch des Christoph Kress.* Kress Archives, deposited in the Archives of the GNM.

[169] Cf. Note 32.

[170] H. Boesch, *Kinderleben in der deutschen Vergangenheit. Monographien zur deutschen Kulturgeschichte* 5 (Leipzig, 1900): 51/52.

[171] A. Butsch (Note 69).

[172] Cf. *Hippolytus Guarinonius (1571–1654): Zur 300. Wiederkehr seines Todestages. Schlern-Schriften* 26 (Innsbruck 1954).

[173] Cf. Note 30, here p. 11/12.

[174] *Ibid., p. 727–29.*

[175] Cf. Note 15.

[176] J. and W. Grimm (Note 12), 11, I, 1 (1952): col. 1702.

[177] Ernst Mummenhoff, 'Geschichtliches über Ackerbau und Gartenwirtschaft in Nürnbergs Umgebung', a lecture given in 1895, publ. in *Gesammelte Aufsätze und Vorträge* (Nuremberg, 1931): 1–92, esp. 36/37, 46.

[178] Cf. Note 30, here p. 11.

[179] Sigrid Flamand-Christensen, *Die männliche Kleidung in der süddeutschen Renaissance* (Berlin, 1934): 10–12; K. Stolleis (Note 40): 55.

[180] Cf. Note 166.

[181] Gerhard Kaufmann, *Stickmustertücher aus dem Besitz des Altonaer Museums. Exhibiton catalogue* (Hamburg, 1975); cf. also the Bibliography, and review by L. v. Wilckens in *Zs. f. Volkskunde* 72 (1976): 156/57.

[182] K. Bräuer (Note 41): 50/51, 82.

[183] Cf. Note 30, here p. 39–168.

[184] *Ibid.: 478/79.*

[185] Cf. Note 166.

[186] A. Ott (Note 109: Plate IV, Fig. 50.

[187] G. Himmelheber, *Spiele. Gesellschaftsspiele aus einem Jahrtausend. Kataloge des Bayer. Nationalmuseums* 14 (Munich and Berlin, 1972): esp. pp. 145 ff., 163 ff.

[188] Cf. Note 166.

[189] Cf. Note 74.

[190] Karl Frommann, 'Eine Christbescherung im Jahre 1619', in *Anz. f. Kunde d. dt. Vorzeit* n.s. 26 (1879): cols. 354–57.

[191] Cf. Note 23.

[192] Cf. Note 25.

[193] Cf. Note 26.

[194] Amelia S. Levetus, 'Dr. Albert Figdor's Collection of Dolls' Furniture', in *The Connoisseur* 35 (1913): 81–88, 37 (1913): 17–25; K.Gröber, Fig. 38–41; L. Bayer, p. 70–72.

[195] Ibid.: 72/73.

[196] Cf. Note 24.

[197] Cf. Note 17.

[198] Muller-Vogelsang pp. 8–19 (on pp. 10–13, the 'Guide' reproduced in translation), Plates I–XXVIII; I. H. van Eeghen, 'Het poppenhuis von Petronella de la Court, huisvrouw van Adam Oortmans', in *Amstelodamum* 47 (1960): 159–67; Marry Veldkamp *Het 17de eeuwse poppenhuis in het Centraal Museum* (Utrecht, 1977).

[199] Zacharias Konrad von Uffenbach (1668–1734), *Merkwürdige Reisen durch Niedersachsen, Holland und Engelland*, 3rd ed. (Ulm, 1754): 648–51.

[200] Muller-Vogelsang, p. 19–21, Plate XXIX–XXXIV; I. H. van Eeghen, 'Het poppenhuis van Petronella Oortman, huisvrouw van Jacob Brandt', in *Amstelodamum* 40 (1953): 113–16; J. H. M. Leeseberg-Terwindt, *Poppenhuizen. Dolls' Houses. Facetten der Verzameling 2. Rijksmuseum* (Amsterdam, 1955): Figs. 8–28.

[201] Muller-Vogelsang, p. 22–25, Plate XXXV; I. H. van Eeghen, 'Het poppenhuis van Margaretha de Ruyter, huisvrouw van Ds Bernardus Somer', in *Amstelodamum* 40 (1953): 137–41; J. H. M. Leeseberg-Terwindt (Note 200): Figs. 1–7.

[202] Beatrice Jansen, *Een rondgang door het poppenhuis. A Guide to the Dolls' House*, 2nd ed. Haags Gemeentemuseum (1977).

[203] Vogelsang-Muller, p. 35–41, Plate XXXVI–XXXIX; *Kind en spel, exhib.* Prinsenhof (Delft, 1953): Cat. No. 109, Figs. 13/14.

[204] Bernard Müller, 'Das Gontard'sche Puppenhaus im Städtischen Museum', in *Alt-Frankfurt* 5 (1913): 1–19.

[205] Henry René d'Allemagne, *Histoire des jouets* (Paris, 1902): 131/32.

[206] K. Gröber, Fig. 152; *Jeux et jouets d'autrefois en Alsace. Exhibition, Musée Alsacien* (Strasbourg, 1976): Cat. No. 13, Plate IV: clay, dried, painted, 16x25x12cm, about 1780.

[207] J. H. M. Leeseberg-Terwindt (Note 200): Figs. 29–32; J. Latham, p. 36.

[208] V. Greene (1979): 87–89, Fig. 56; E. King, p. 167–72.

[209] V. Greene (1979): 89/90, 99, Fig. 57.

[210] Ibid.: 99/100, Fig. 58; E. King, p. 165.

[211] J. Latham, p. 163–70; E. King, p. 172–4.

[212] V. Greene (1979): 118/19, Fig. 74/75; E. King, p. 174–8.

[213] V. Greene (1979): 108, 117/18, Fig. 72/73.

[214] Ibid., p. 122/3, Fig. 79/80.

[215] Ibid., p. 50, Fig. 16.

[216] F. Gill Jacobs, p. 126–28, Fig. 40–43; E. King, p. 195.

[217] K. Gröber, Fig. 65/66; F. Gill Jacobs, p. 137/38, Fig. 45/46; E. King, p. 184, 186.

[218] K. Gröber, *Das Puppenhaus der Fürstin Augusta Dorothea von Schwarzburg-Arnstadt, Der Eiserne Hammer* 6 (Königstein/Ts., 1934); Wolfgang Leber, *Die Puppenstadt Mon Plaisir.* (Museen der Stadt Arnstadt, 1975).

[219] Georg Hieronymus Bestelmeyer (d. 1852), *Pädagogisches Magazin zur lehrreichen und angenehmen Unterhaltung der Jugend* (Nuremberg, 1793 ff.); later called *Magazin von verschiedenen Kunst– und anderen nützlichen Sachen* Parts 1–9; with 'new and improved' editions of each Part appearing soon afterwards.

[220] Full details, with documentation and literature, in Manfred Bachmann's *Das Waldkirchner Spielzeugmusterbuch* (Leipzig, also Munich, 1977); cf. also Karl Ewald Fritzsch, 'Motive des Spielzeugs nach erzgebirgischen Musterbüchern des 19. Jahrhunderts', in *Sächs. Heimatbll.* 11 (1965): 499–576, with 81 illustrations.

[221] On the occasion of the Nuremberg Toy Fair in 1978, Dieter Hasselblatt wrote in *Frankfurter Allgemeine Zeitung*, 25.2.1978, that today 'the (toy) trade sees play and games entirely as something trivial and incidental . . . , and not (as) stimulation of the imagination and of creativity'.

[222] J. Latham, pp. 29, 183; V. Greene (1979): 199; E. King, pp. 236, 241–2.

[223] Clifford Musgrave, *Queen Mary's Dolls' House* (London, 1967).

[224] *Titania's Palace.* Illustrated Catalogue. Auction, Christie, Manson & Woods Ltd. London 10.1.1978.

A selection of general literature on dolls' houses, in chronological order.

Samuel Muller and Willem Vogelsang, *Holländische Patrizierhäuser* (Utrecht, 1909). Referred to as Muller-Vogelsang.

Karl Gröber, *Kinderspielzeug aus alter Zeit. Eine Geschichte des Spielzeugs* (Berlin, 1928). Referred to as K. Gröber.

Flora Gill Jacobs, *A History of Dolls' Houses. Four Centuries of Domestic World in Miniature* (New York, 1953). Referred to as F. Gill Jacobs.

Vivien Greene, *English Dolls' Houses of the Eighteenth and Nineteenth Centuries* (London, 1955 and 1979). Referred to as V. Greene.

Leonie von Wilckens, *Tageslauf im Puppenhaus. Bürgerliches Leben vor dreihundert Jahren* (Munich, 1956). Referred to as L. v. Wilckens.

Lydia Bayer, *Das europäische Puppenhaus von 1550–1800. Geschichte und Formen, ein Spiegelbild der gleichzeitigen Wohnkultur.* Diss. (Würzburg, 1962 – part printed). Referred to as L. Bayer.

Jean Latham, *Dolls' Houses. A Personal Choice* (London 1973). Referred to as J. Latham.

Vivien Greene, *Family Dolls' Houses* (London, 1973).

Eileen King, *Dolls and Dolls' Houses* (London 1977) (German ed. Zurich, 1977). Referred to as E. King.

Index

Photographs

Photographs are by Helga Schmidt-Glassner, of Stuttgart.
The following have also been included:

Altonaer Museum, Hamburg   266
Gemeentemuseum, The Hague   Fig. 25
Germanisches Nationalmuseum, Nuremberg
  Figs. 1-5, Figs. 7-24, Fig. 26, Fig. 27, Fig. 29.
The Museum of London   159
Nuremberg Toy Catalogue   Fig. 28
Rijksmuseum, Amsterdam   96-104
Staatliche Graphische Sammlung, Munich   Fig.6

The Plates

Nuremberg Baby House dated 1611
Nuremberg, Germanisches Nationalmuseum
Photographs 1–13

◁ 2   The date, 1611, may be seen above the window painted on the wall as part of a scene showing people dining and playing cards

1   (*page 73*) In addition to the three main stories, there is a cellar and an attic

3 Painted on the cellar door is a maid taking a child, who is already undressed, to the bathroom

4 Against the wall in the yard stands a painted well where water may be drawn for the flower gardens

5 Gilded balusters form part of the balustrades around the yard

6 The privy is under the stairs

7 Doors with architectonic frame-
work open onto the rooms on either
side of the landing ▷

8 Hunting scenes, pictures of
maids and young troopers decorate
the walls of the staircase

9 In the room on the second floor left, with its magnificent baroque bed, some items were added after 1800 (*see photograph No. 227*)

10 The state room on the other hand is seventeenth century ▷

11, 12   When the sitting-room was 'modernized' in the middle of the eighteenth century, the garlands painted at the top of the walls and the ceiling panelling were left undisturbed

13   The large wall painting in the room on the ground floor is partly based on an engraving by Jan Sadeler the Elder (*see Fig. 3*)

12 △

13 ▽

Nuremberg Baby House of 1639
Nuremberg, Germanisches
National-museum
Photographs 14–31

15   So far, it has not been possible to establish that the lion in the lattice of the oval window is an armorial beast from the arms of the original owner

16   The stable is entered by its own side-door   ▷

◁ 14   A house well-preserved in every respect. The date appears on the central dormer

17 To the left of the basement are a storage room and maid's room on top, with the stable and wine cellar below

18 On the right are the nursery and another maid's room, and below them the shop with office and the laundry

19 The scales, with several sets of weights, and the household-board, come from the kitchen ▷

20 The 'journal' and 'account book' are both dated 1640

19 △

20 ▽

21 Above the wainscot are pictures of Our Lady and allegorical personifications of the Virtues

22 Child's cot, hanging cradle, child's chair and walker belong in the nursery

23 The well-filled linen-press stands on the first-floor landing

24 The state room has an even more pretentious coffered ceiling than the sitting-room

25 The small meat-safe has two airholes covered with wire-netting at the side

26 △

27 ▽

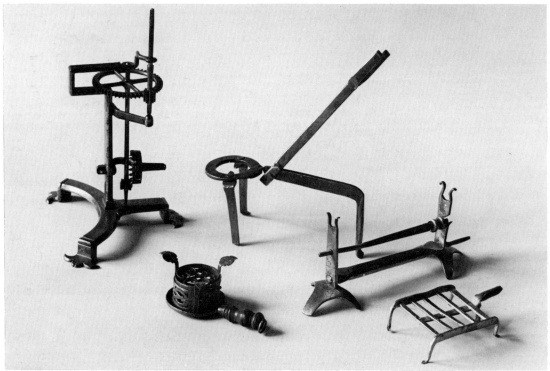

26 The wainscoting leaves space for the tiled stove

27, 28 In the kitchen, cooking continued to be done over an open fire for a long time. This required a roaster, tripod, and turn-spit; a chafing dish provided limited heat

29 The comb-bag holds brushes and combs; it is decorated as richly as the mirror frame

30 A copper warming pan is standing on the floor beside the washstand

31 The close-stool has not been forgotten; it is placed next to the bed with its green silk curtains and piled-high bedding ▷

Nuremberg Dolls' Cabinet from
the seventeenth century
Nuremberg, Germanisches Nationalmuseum
Photographs 32–36, 42, 43

32 It was not only in bedrooms that beds were to be found

33 A spacious kitchen and a sitting-room above it

34 The kitchen has utensils and dishes of pewter and copper, brass and iron, wood and earthenware

35, 36   The fan-shaped dishes with their blue decoration are of Nuremberg faience

37   Accurate craftsmanship has produced the stand for the lace pillow, the yarn-winder and reels

38, 39 Pewter jugs and wooden boxes are miniature replicas in every detail

40, 41 The turner has put all his efforts into making these spinning wheels real masterpieces in miniature

42 The tall stove of green glazed tiles is particularly magnificent

43 Moulded and flaming fillets decorate the cupboard ▷

*Nuremberg Baby House from
the late seventeenth century
Nuremberg, Germanisches Nationalmuseum (on loan
from the Bäumler family)
Photographs 44–53*

44 In the shop, not only groceries and medicines are for sale, but all kinds of paper as well

45 In this House, one must imagine the stairs to be hidden at the back

46 The door at the back of the stable leads to the servant's room

45 △

46 ▽

47 Inside and out, the House now shows the original paint with a dark red ground, hidden until recently under a later coat of cream paint

48 The only House to have bottle-glass windows at the sides, with muted light entering the room

49 The portraits on the cornices date back to the early eighteenth century

50 The baskets probably came from the Lichtenfels region

48 △

49 ▽

51 The tin coach was added during the nineteenth century

52 A woodworker's bench stands behind the wheelbarrow

53 The painted walls relate the yard to the vista of a garden painted in deep perspective at the back

51 △

53 ▽

Nuremberg Baby House from the seventeenth–eighteenth centuries
formerly owned by the Kress von Kressenstein family
Nuremberg, Germanisches Nationalmuseum
Photographs 54–59

◁ 54 The Table, charmingly inlaid with ivory, is set for a festive meal

55 The two gables apparently did not originally form part of this House ▷

Pages 104 and 105:
56, 57 All the rooms have a low balustrade at the front. The House is peopled by dolls with wax heads from the eighteenth century

58, 59   The chairs in the sitting-room have seats and backs embroidered in tent stitch

Nuremberg Baby House of 1673
London, Bethnal Green
Museum
Photographs 60 and 61

60 The front consists of two doors that open

61 The state kitchen has two closets at the back; above it and the kitchen proper are a bedroom and a sitting-room

60 △   61 ▽

62 The spinet can still be played. It belongs to the 1639 Nuremberg Baby House (*see photographs 14–31*) *Nuremberg, Germanisches National-museum*

63 The folding screen covered with brocade paper comes from the same House, but dates back only to the early eighteenth century *Nuremberg, Germanisches National-museum*

64 Colourful painted decor on cupboards was popular as early as the seventeenth century *Nuremberg, Germanisches National-museum*

62 △

63 ▽

64 △

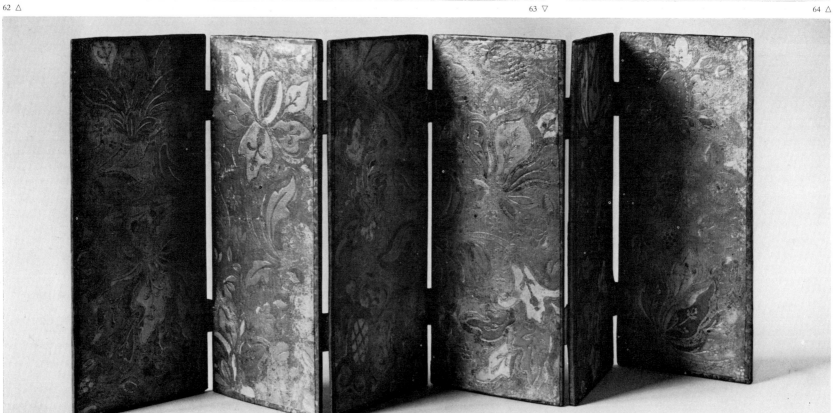

*Two Nuremberg Dolls' Rooms
with Kitchen
first half of
seventeenth century
Nuremberg, Germanisches
National-museum
Photographs 65, 67–69*

65 Many kitchens had a special cage for poultry

66 The carved head-board of the Swiss doll's bed bears the inscription 'Wan Gott mit uns/wer will wider uns' (If God with us, who will be against us)
Zurich, Schweizerisches Landes-museum

67 The woodwork, the textiles and the paintings made this tester-bed a real showpiece (see also No. 69)

68 The cupboard is rather similar to the furniture in the state room of the 1611 Nuremberg Baby House (*see No. 10*)

66 △   67 △   68 ▽

69   The medallions on the inside of
the tester show scenes from the Bible
(*see also No. 67*)

70

Strasbourg Baby House, about 1680
Strasbourg, Musée de l'Oeuvre de Notre Dame
Photographs 70–76

71 Four rooms are accommodated in a cupboard with high base

◁ 70 Above the tiled stove, a drying rack is suspended from the ceiling in the sitting-room

72 Downstairs are the sitting-room and the yard complete with stable; above the kitchen and a second sitting-room

71 △   72 ▽

73 The Alsatian furniture is much decorated

74 In the cobbled yard, a trap door leads to the cellar

75 The kitchen and the upstairs sitting-room have windows at the back

Basle Baby House,
late seventeenth century
Basle, Historisches Museum
im Haus zum Kirschgarten
Photographs 77–84

78 The chandelier has two tiers of candles

◁ 77 Three rooms are built into a cupboard with a door; the height of the cupboard is 152cm

79, 80 In the sitting-room, the wainscot and the part of the wall above are painted with flowers and branches

81 The baroque cupboard from the Upper Rhine has three mighty twisted columns

82 The back of the cellar has been partitioned off; here, wine barrels are kept, whilst the firewood is on the right

83 In the kitchen, the walls are tiled to half their height

84 The stove of green-glazed pottery, bearing the date 1768, has been added only recently ▷

85 The dolls' kitchen with its hearth of different top levels belonged to a St Gallen family; it shows that kitchens remained more or less the same until about the middle of the nineteenth century *Zurich, Schweizerisches Landesmuseum*

86   The art cabinet is full of precious works of art and rarities

◁ 87 In this 'House', which is built into a cabinet, the most distinguished rooms are on the first floor

88 A water chamber and a *'secreet'* are built in at the back of the kitchen

89 In the lying-in room, the pictures, either painted or carved in ivory, complete with frames, are just as valuable as the various items of porcelain

90 Landscapes by Frederick de Moucheron cover the walls of the reception room

91 Three maids are at work in the linen room under the roof

92 Carved ivory figures representing Faith and Hope decorate the doors of the cabinet

93 Ivory reliefs with scenes from the Passion surround a representation of the Last Judgment

94 The master, wearing a comfortable dressing-gown, is sitting at his desk in the entresol, surrounded by records and folios

95 The bedroom has a magnificent silk furnishing

Margaretha de Ruyter's Baby House
Amsterdam, fourth quarter of the seventeenth century
Amsterdam, Rijksmuseum
Photographs 96–98

96, 97 The walls of the lying-in room are covered in a red chintz, as is the bed with its bunches of feathers. The contemporary dolls are kept as inhabitants

98 As the more distinguished rooms on the first floor, the lying-in room and the best parlour have higher ceilings ▷

Petronella Oortman's Baby House, Amsterdam, end of seventeenth century
Amsterdam, Rijksmuseum

Photographs 99–104

99 Painting of the House by Jacob Appel (1680–1751), early eighteenth century
Amsterdam, Rijksmuseum

100 Nicolaas Piemont painted the wide open landscapes for the walls of the reception room

◁ 99   100 △

1 The painted top of the folding
le is 24cm in length

2 A painting by J. Voorhout de-
ates the chimney-piece of this
m with its embroidered wall
gings   ▷

101 ▽   102 ▷

103 The lying-in room has wainscoting and, built-in, a wardrobe and an alcove bed

104 Dutch housewives, like Nuremberg ladies, took pride in their state kitchen, where the best pieces were on display

Sara Ploos van Amstel's Baby House, Amsterdam, 1743
The Hague, Gemeentemuseum
Photographs 105–131

105   The Baby House is accommodated in a cupboard with three drawers in its base

106   When the doors are open, the 'House', combining older and later elements, is on view

105 △   106 ▽

109, 111, 114 The linen cupboard in the lying-in room is almost of the same design as the cupboard housing the whole 'House' (see also Nos. 105 and 106); the dolls in this room were given some new clothes in 1743

110 Again the most distinguished rooms are on the first floor, but the lying-in room is not included among them

112, 113 The walls and ceiling of the first-floor vestibule have been painted to suggest plaster work

109 △   110 ▽

111 △   112 △   113 △   114 ▽

115 △

116 △

117 △

118 ▽

115 The kitchen contains Delft-ware and Japanese porcelain as well as stoneware

116 Some of the metal utensils are made of silver

117, 118 All kinds of basket ware, plaited in different patterns

120 △   121 △   122 ▽

120　Looking at this silver filigree box, one might forget its tiny dimensions

121　The oval table top has a lacquer paint in late seventeenth century 'chinoiserie' style

122　Mrs Ploos van Amstel had the harpsichord case repainted

123 The walls of the music room
are decorated with open landscapes;
the room is lit by six silver sconces

124, 125 In the china cabinet are displayed Dutch imitations in opaque glass of the popular blue and white Chinese porcelain and also blanc de chine pieces with their delicate embossed decoration; the tall mirrors on the side walls multiply these treasures

126 An older collector's cabinet
has been built into the back wall of
the china cabinet

127   Playing cards, dice with their cup, a chessboard and a clay pipe

128   Even the many different kitchen utensils are select

129   Silver utensils for the fireplace and for lighting the room

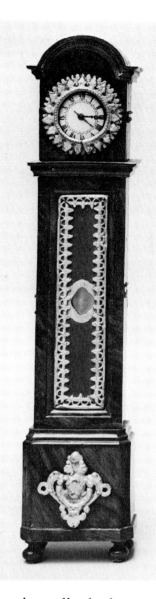

130 In the tall clock-case on the landing a watch tells the time; the cabinet houses a collection of sea-shells

131 The bottles in the silver cooler are typical Dutch shapes of the late seventeenth century

Baby House from the Blaauw Collection,
middle of the eighteenth century
Haarlem, Stedelijk Museum
Photographs 132–135

132 The room known as the chapel, on the first floor

133 The outer and the inner doors of the cupboard have to be opened to present the Baby House with its four floors (the lower floor is not shown here)   ▷

134 The far right-hand corner of the dining room

135 Silver is displayed in the alcove at the back of the dining room

The Gontard Baby House,
seventeenth–nineteenth centuries
Frankfurt-on-Main, Historisches Museum
Photographs 136–143

136   The stand and frame were not
made before the middle of the
nineteenth century

137   This House shows particularly
well the change while used by
different generations over a period
of 200 years

136 △   137 ▽

147

138 The baroque garden vista on the wall of what is now a storeroom points to apparent changes

139 The tiled stove and at least the layout of the cupboard belong to the seventeenth century furnishings of the bedroom

◁ 141 A wine-press stands next to the linen-press on the upper landing

142 The baroque painted ceiling with its moulded cornice hardly goes with the kitchen below

144 The Palladian front of this Baby House belongs to the early eighteenth century *Oxford, Vivien Greene's collection*

145–149 Sarah Fetherstonhaugh's House, about 1740 *Uppark*

145, 146 All the rooms have white panelling; the table utensils are of silver

147 Each of the nine rooms has its own 'door' that can be opened in the façade of this House

148 A lying-in room is also commonly found in the English Baby Houses

149 The rooms in the basement are very low-ceilinged

145 △

146 ▽

148 △

149 ▽

150–152, 156 The Tate Family House, about 1760
London, Bethnal Green Museum

150–152 The external design is based on Dorset houses of that period

151 As with the Blackett House, which is about twenty years older, (see No. 157), stairs placed before the basement lead to the main entrance on the first floor

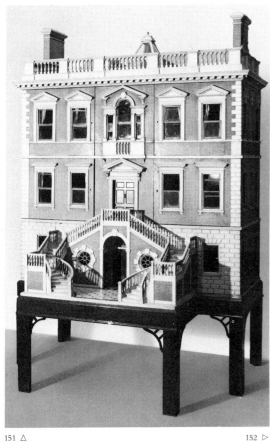

151 △   152 ▷

153-155 The only difference between these pieces of furniture from English Baby Houses and their full-size counterparts of about 1650–1700 is one of scale
London, Bethnal Green Museum

153 △

154 ▽

156 The furnishings of the Tate Baby House (last third of eighteenth century) were modernized in about 1830

157–159 The Blackett Baby House,
about 1740–5
Museum of London

157 As in the Dutch Baby Houses
the hearth is built into the wall like a
fireplace

158, 159 The House is marked by
its painted wallpapers

◁ 157   158 △

160 △

162

160 This plain Dolls' House from the late eighteenth century also has a front that opens in sections

161 This is not a dolls' house, but a child's wardrobe made in 1709
London, Bethnal Green Museum

162 The front door of the Cane End Baby House (see also No. 252)
Oxford, Vivien Greene's collection

161 ▽

163 A house of c. 1830, unusual because of the high parapet composed of balustrading, reminiscent of what in New England would be called 'the Widows' walk', where women would look out to sea for their husbands' ships.
Oxford, Vivien Greene's collection ▷

164 △

165 ▽

166 ▽

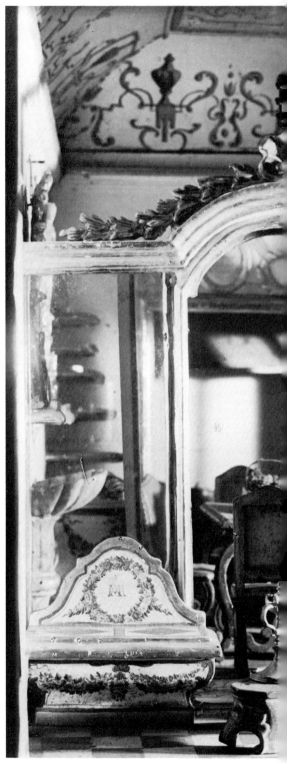

164–168 Single-storied and open to view from all sides, this represents a distinguished palazzo in Bologna; the furniture and fittings are carved, painted, and partly gilded

*'Mon Plaisir', the Dolls' Town
of Princess Augusta Dorothea
von Schwarzburg
First half of
eighteenth century
Arnstadt, Schlossmuseum
Photographs 169–191*

169, 170   A lively market scene, at
two levels

171   A farm-cart is bringing bags of flour to the bakery

172, 175   The weaver at work below, the turner above; the wives are assisting their husbands

173   The apothecary's shop is stocked with the necessary ingredients and products to make up the doctor's prescriptions

174   A ragged beggarwoman is asking the butcher's wife for a handout

171 △

173 ▽

174 △   175 ▽

176 On the farm, the young couple are at breakfast; a woman is making butter

177 Coaches are stopping at the residence; the princess is alighting from a sedan-chair

178   To the right of the tea-table, a lady is sitting at her embroidery frame

179   The court kitchen is situated above the wine-cellar   ▷

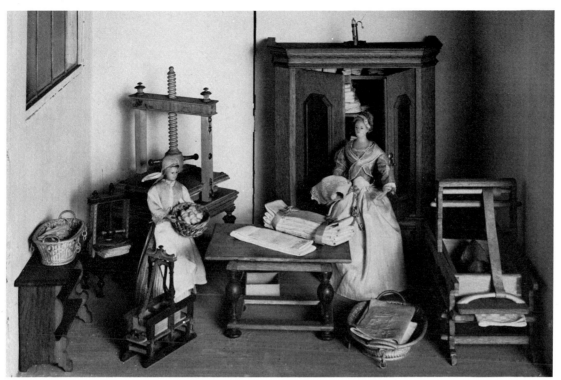

180 The housekeeper in the linen room at the residence may be recognised by the two large keys at her belt

181 The residence is obviously more expensively and lavishly furnished than the middle-class and working-class homes

182, 183 A nanny is also in charge of the nursery in the middle-class home but, in the residence, even some of the maids are wearing silk gowns

184 In the dressing room at the bottom left, maidservants are attending the lady at her toilet; in the room on the right, the court hairdresser is in attendance; and in the nursery upstairs the new-born child is brought to the princess ▷

185   Figures from the popular Italian Comedy are depicted on two of the small tables

186   Naturally the miniature residence also has its mirror and china cabinet

187   While dining alone, the princess listens to a report   ▷

185 △   186 ▽

188   A game of cards is in progress on the left, whilst on the right positions are taken for the dance

189   The fireplace with its tall tiled chimneybreast recalls those in Dutch Baby Houses

190 Time was whiled away with all kinds of games, chess, draughts, mill, and backgammon

191 Much pleasure was gained in the theatre; here, a band of dwarfs is playing

192, 193 Large cupboards for plates and other ware could be entered in eighteenth century Nuremberg
Nuremberg, Germanisches National-museum

194 This simple rococo room belonged to the barons von Holz-schuher, a patrician family in Nuremberg
Nuremberg, Germanisches National-museum

192 △

194 ▽

195 The country-style bed in the Ulm Baby House (see No. 197) has been added at a later date
Ulm, Museum der Stadt Ulm

196 The small chest of drawers on the left has been decorated with coloured paper, that on the right is painted; eighteenth century
Nuremberg, Germanisches National-museum

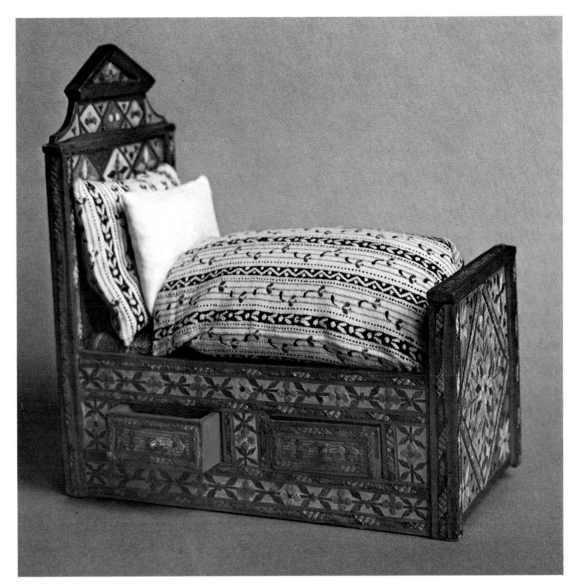

Baby House, seventeenth–nineteenth centuries
Ulm, Museum der Stadt Ulm
Photographs 197–205

197 The ten differently furnished rooms have been put together in recent times

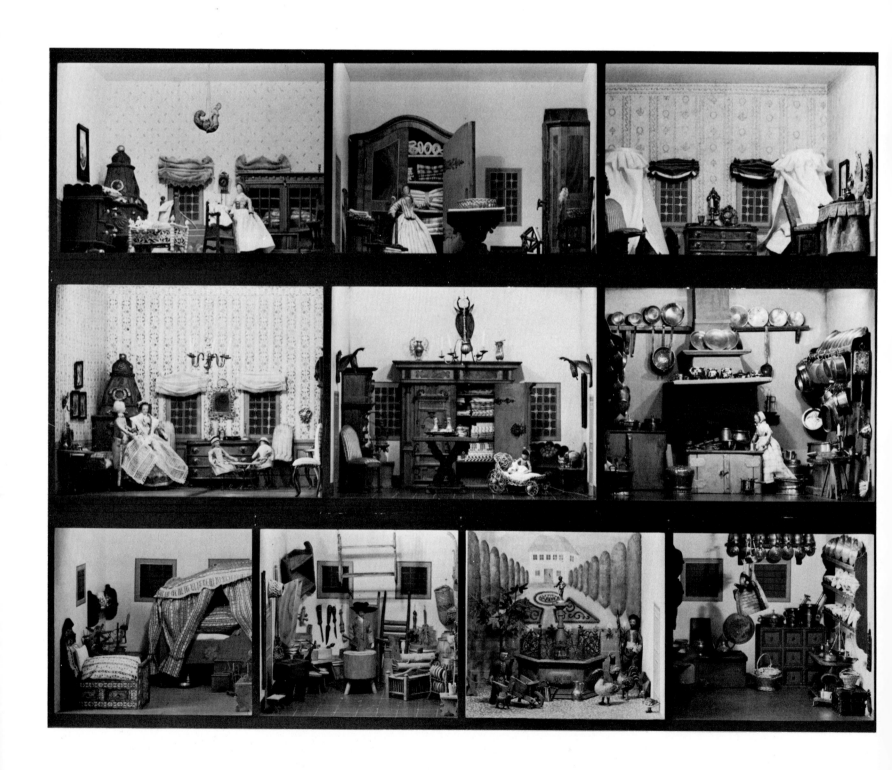

198 A cooper's workshop

199 The fountain in the garden
bears the date 1748

198 △

199 ▽

201　The Swabian linen press with
its three pillars in front dates back to
the seventeenth century

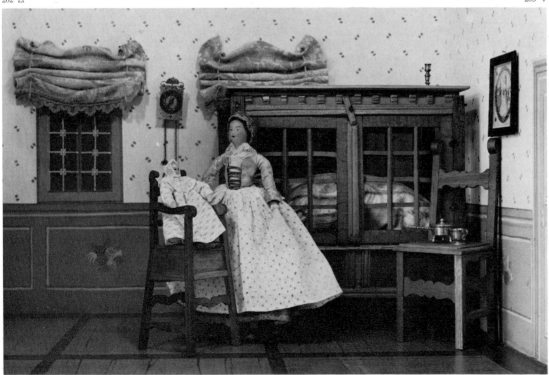

202, 203, 205 The dolls have new clothes, and furniture more in country-style has been added in some rooms

204 The female figure of the chandelier is one of the older pieces

204 ▽   205 ▷

Lying-in rooms from late eighteenth-century Alsace Strasbourg, Musée Alsacien Photographs 206, 207

206, 207 The Alsatian miniature rooms with their clay figures–celebrating the christening beside the mother's bed–reflect an old tradition that is also evident in the lying-in rooms found in Dutch and some English Baby Houses

Toyshops from the eighteenth and early nineteenth centuries
Photographs 208–226, 231

208 This plain box, decorated with paper rosettes, contains one of the oldest toyshops (see also No. 214)
Nuremberg, Germanisches National-museum

209 Milliner's shops of the early nineteenth century had everything a lady or gentleman could want in that line
Nuremberg, Germanisches National-museum

208 △

209 ▽

210, 211 The brightly-embroidered purses bear several dates from the first ten years of the nineteenth century (*see also No. 209*)
Nuremberg, Germanisches National-museum

212, 213 Painted with flowers on the outside, this eighteenth-century shop from Switzerland already offers some almost 'real' goods
Zurich, Schweizerisches Landes-museum

214 Here, painted blocks of wood represent the goods (*see also No. 208*)
Nuremberg, Germanisches National-museum

215–217 The second of these two milliner's shops in Nuremberg and Munich bears the date 1805
Nuremberg, Germanisches National-museum (No. 215)
Munich, Münchner Stadtmuseum (Nos. 216, 217)

◁ 218 The hat-shop, about 1830 –40, has been stocked later; the doll only arrived early in the twentieth century
Rüschlikon, Annet Beyer's collection

219 In the *Industrie-Magazin*, shoes and hats share the premises
Kommern, Rheinisches Freilichtmuseum

220 This simple shop from the late Biedermeier period is housed in a box and has two doors to be locked
Munich, Münchner Stadtmuseum

219 △

220 ▽

221 At the grocers, one can also buy birch brooms and quite a variety of ropes and cords
Überlingen, Heimatmuseum (Johanna Kunz's collection)

222 After the weight of the goods is determined on the scales, the price is rung up on the cash register which first made its appearance at the turn of the nineteenth century
Überlingen, Heimatmuseum (Johanna Kunz's collection)

223 A rather impressive shop for wax products from the middle of the nineteenth century (*see also No. 231*)
Munich, Münchner Stadtmuseum

224 Zintl's store from Kempten
has survived with all its contents; it
dates back to 1875–80
Munich, Münchner Stadtmuseum

225 This shop with its fabrics, silk ribbons and knitting wool was probably intended to serve country people
Augsburg, Städtische Kunstsammlungen

226 Butchers' shops are an English speciality. The one from Swanton Road, Bow, in London, is reproduced here
London, Bethnal Green Museum

225 △

226 ▽

227 A new white stove was put into the 1611 Nuremberg Baby House (*see also No. 9*) after 1800
Nuremberg, Germanisches National-museum

228, 230 Two clocks of the same period in Nuremberg Baby Houses
Nuremberg, Germanisches National-museum

229 This stove of severely classical form belongs to the Augsburg Baby House (*see also Nos. 232, 233*)
Augsburg, Städtische Kunstsammlungen

*Dolls' Houses and Rooms
from Western Europe,
about 1800–60
Photographs 232–265*

232, 233 Augsburg Baby House,
early nineteenth century. In the low
base, the garden adjoins the yard;
the spacious kitchen is situated two
floors higher.
Augsburg, Städtische Kunstsammlungen

234, 235 A well-equipped kitchen
also has its storeroom for all kinds of
ware
*Augsburg, Städtische Kunstsamm-
lungen* ▷

234 △ 235 ▽

237 In Germany, serial production of dolls' house furnishings started during the first third of the nineteenth century
Rüschlikon, Annet Beyer's collection

238 An upper middle-class House from Basle, middle of the nineteenth century
Zurich, Weber Collection

◁ 236 Until well into the nineteenth century, dishes were arranged on open shelves all the way up the walls
Augsburg, Städtische Kunstsammlungen

239   A Biedermeier room with sofa and table in one corner and the bed behind a folding screen in the other, built into a house-like box
Munich, Münchner Stadtmuseum

240   The handsome walnut furniture in this late Biedermeier room was later complemented with bric-a-brac of a slightly later date
Munich, Münchner Stadtmuseum

241   The Alsatian rocking bed is so large compared to the other furniture that at the least it must have been intended for an older child among the dolls
Strasbourg, Musée Alsacien

242 This French dolls' house is open to view from several sides on the lower floor; it was probably not intended as a plaything for children *Paris, Musée des Arts Décoratifs*

243–245 An English dolls' house from the early nineteenth century. The neo-Gothic style also left its mark on dolls' houses in England. The amazing front hardly leads one to expect the division into three floors inside. The two towers contain six smaller rooms
Oxford, Vivien Greene's collection

246 The fireplace is covered by a
sheet cast in iron
Oxford, Vivien Greene's collection

247 The silver tea-set on its silver
tray is essential in an English dolls'
house
Oxford, Vivien Greene's collection

248 The hall from c. 1900 occupies
two stories, with steep stairs leading
to the upper rooms
Oxford, Vivien Greene's collection ▷

249, 251　In about 1810, in England certain neo-classicist features are combined with the neo-Gothic style
Oxford, Vivien Greene's collection

250　This room from the second quarter of the eighteenth century contains some later pieces of equipment (*see Nos. 162 and 269*)
Oxford, Vivien Greene' collection

252　The drawingroom of the Gothic Castle shown in Plates 243 –245, first quarter of the nineteenth century.
Oxford, Vivien Greene's collection

249 △

250 ▽

253, 254 About 1850, English façades still show neo-classicist details, but are rather elongated
Oxford, Vivien Greene's collection

255 During the second half of the
nineteenth century, more and more
dolls' houses were made to be
looked at from at least three sides
Oxford, Vivien Greene's collection

256 A greenhouse has been placed in the angle made by two partly half-timbered (imitation) walls
Oxford, Vivien Greene's collection

257 A portico with columns is typical for an English façade
Oxford, Vivien Greene's collection

THE ORIGINAL SWAN

258 The stairs leading up to the front door of Lady Lansdowne's House (1860) resemble those seen in the middle of the eighteenth century (*see also Nos. 151, 159*)
Museum of London

259 A three-storied London town-house, about 1840–50, from South Kensington
London, Bethnal Green Museum

260-262 In about 1835-8, the wife and daughters of John Egerton Killer, physician in Manchester, furnished the living room and kitchen below, and a second living room and a bedroom above, in a lacquered cabinet
London, Bethnal Green Museum

263 The dressing table from Mrs Bryant's Baby House (Nos. 275-278), about 1860
London, Bethnal Green Museum ▷

260 △   261 △   262 ▽

264 The living room in Mrs Drew's House, about 1860–5
London, Bethnal Green Museum

265 The Library or 'Study' of 'The Whiteway', c. 1845–50. Letters personally delivered were folded in this 'cocked-hat' style before the general use of envelopes
Oxford, Vivien Greene's collection

264 △

265 ▽

266 The Smarje family's dolls' kitchen is housed in a carved box from the middle of the eighteenth century
Hamburg, Altonaer Museum

267   One of the advances of the late nineteenth century is the free-standing stove. This enamelled example was manufactured by Maerklin about 1900
Zurich, Weber collection

268, 270 Two kitchens from the middle of the nineteenth century
Kommern, Rheinisches Freilichtmuseum (*No. 268*)
Munich, Münchner Stadtmuseum (*No. 270*)

269 Like the 1680 Dutch Baby House at Utrecht (*No. 88*), this English kitchen has a built-in hearth
Oxford, Vivien Greene's collection

268 △   269 △   270 ▽

271 The stepped stove – like the one in the St Gallen kitchen (*No. 85*) – is of glazed pottery, with embossed decorations at the side
Kommern, Rheinisches Freilichtmuseum

272 A privy has been built into the corner of the kitchen
Kommern, Rheinisches Freilichtmuseum

273, 274 The small free-standing tin stoves almost disappear among the ware still arrayed on open shelves and the utensils hanging on the walls
Überlingen, Heimatmuseum (Johanna Kunz's collection)

275–278 The dolls' house Mrs Bryant of Oakenshaw had made and furnished in 1860 is a true-to-life cabinet piece (*see also No. 263*) *London, Bethnal Green Museum*

279–281 In about 1845–50, the painter Ludwig Adam Kelterborn of Basle had a dolls' house made for his three daughters, in a cupboard with doors at the front and back, and windows at the sides
Basle, Historisches Museum im Haus zum Kirschgarten

282   A three-storied front from the
period of Historism
Rüschlikon, Annet Beyer's collection

283   Transfers decorate the façade
of this Nuremberg dolls' house,
about 1875–80
Munich, Münchner Stadtmuseum   ▷

284 This room contains besides tiny furniture, much ware and many utensils, also several samplers and other examples of needlework, mostly embroidery and lace
Kommern, Rheinisches Freilichtmuseum

285, 286 The owners of this dolls' house from the late nineteenth century have gradually added various items
Burg Lahneck

287, 289 Rooms in the Old German style from about 1890; furniture with fretwork decoration was popular. The cupboards in Munich and Augsburg come from the same series which also included tables and chairs, wall-clocks and dressing tables, picture frames, and even door and window frames

Munich, Münchner Stadtmuseum (No. 287)
Augsburg, Städtische Kunstsammlungen (No. 289)

288 Bottle-glass in the bow-window supports the Old German character
Kommern, Rheinisches Freilichtmuseum

287 △

288 ▽

290 △   291 ▽   292 △

290 The furnishings of the class-room also reflect the predominant taste
Stuttgart, private ownership

291 This was indeed how the girls of the third year would be sitting in their classroom at Altona in 1880
Hamburg, Altonaer Museum

292 In this Old German Room, Martin Luther and his family are gathered around the Christmas tree
London, Bethnal Green Museum

293 Fretwork decorations even adorn the small house-altar
Kommern, Rheinisches Freilicht-museum
▷

294, 295, 297, 298 From the third quarter of the century onwards, heavy oak furniture, well-upholstered and covered in velvet, was popular for dolls' houses, but also items with gold paint imitating the Boulle technique of about 1700
Zürich, Weber collection (No. 294)
Kommern, Rheinisches Freilichtmuseum (No. 295)
Strasbourg, Musée Alsacien (No. 297)
Überlingen, Heimatmuseum (Johanna Kunz's collection) (No. 298)

296 A dolls' confectioner's shop
Hamburg, Altonaer Museum ▷

296 ▽   297 △   298 ▽

299 This Dolls' house of about 1900 has a balcony above the covered porch
Kommern, Rheinisches Freilichtmuseum

300 Draped transparent curtains, a delicate cover on the centre table, long fringes on the rug in front of the sofa – all these are characteristic of the well-cared-for sitting-room from the turn of the century
Überlingen, Heimatmuseum (Johanna Kunz's collection)

301, 302 The grand piano is a Blüthner; next to it are pieces of neo-rococo furniture. This is the older Nuremberg house (*see also No. 283*)
Munich, Münchner Stadtmuseum

300 △

301 ▽

302 ▽

303 △

303–305 Table lamps, family photos, children's furniture, a flower stand and fireplace furniture also complete the equipment of a dolls' house
Zurich, Weber Collection (Nos. 303, 305)
Stuttgart, private ownership (No. 304)

304 ▽

306 Punched-out gilded metal borders frame the wall panels; the salon from about 1890 also has heavy, draped curtains
Munich, Münchner Stadtmuseum

307, 308   Mirror salon in the house
shown in No. 282
Rüschlikon, Annet Beyer's collection

309   A living room in the Old German
style, about 1900
Überlingen, Heimatmuseum (Johanna Kunz's collection)

307 △   308 △   309 ▽

310, 311 Elsewhere, the furniture
at that time was neo-classicist
Zurich, Weber Collection

312, 313 Some furniture was in Art Nouveau style, other pieces followed styles from the second half of the eighteenth century (*see also Nos. 301, 302*)
Überlingen, Heimatmuseum (Johanna Kunz's collection)

315–317 Art Nouveau brought more graceful and exotically col-oured furniture
Überlingen, Heimatmuseum (Johanna Kunz's collection)

318 △

318 From the 1890s onwards, country-style painted furniture also influenced that in the dolls' houses
Stuttgart, private collection

319–322 During the later nineteenth century, child-like dolls began to take the place of doll ladies. Dolls' rooms then also came frequently to be nurseries with white-painted furniture
Überlingen, Heimatmuseum (Johanna Kunz's collection)

319 ▽

320 △

321 △

322 ▽

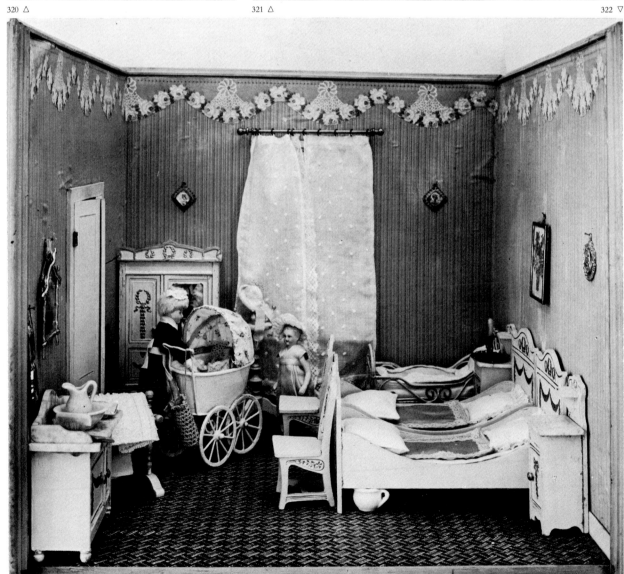

323, 324 The dolls' kitchen and the model for the 'first school kitchen to be established by the city of Munich in 1895' are so realistic that one almost forgets they are toys
Munich, Münchner Stadtmuseum

※ IM HAUSE DAS BESTE, SIND HEITERE GASTE. ※